Clarity Before Crisis

Beyond Financial, Legal, and Healthcare Guidance for Aging, Caregiving, and Family Legacy

by

Benjamin Bolen, CFP®

Dedication

For the caregiver

Table of Contents

Author's Note

The Clarity System

This book is the foundation of the Clarity System, a comprehensive framework designed to help families prepare for crises before they strike. The pages you're holding introduce the stories, strategies, and core tools. If this book is read and then collects dust on a shelf, it will have failed its purpose. This is not simply a book to inform; it's a framework to implement. To gain the most from it, you will need to put it into practice. Each chapter concludes with specific action steps designed to move you forward. Alongside these pages, a complete package of guides, worksheets, and updated resources is available at **Claritybeforecrisis.com**. These tools are designed to help you apply the insights from the page to your family conversations, professional planning, and daily decisions.

There, you can download our full resource library, including:

- **The Master Checklist** – step-by-step tasks for organizing finances, legal documents, and care decisions.
- **Family Care Meeting Guide** – scripts and structure for leading difficult but vital conversations.
- **Caregiver Worksheet** – tools for coordinating roles, duties, and respite.
- **Personal Care Plan** – a document to capture your healthcare wishes, daily living, and quality of life.
- **Legacy Wealth Scorecard** – a framework to measure true wealth across finances, health, relationships, and time.

- **Business Owner Succession Guide** – how to plan exit and succession to help ensure legacy and maximize enterprise value

These resources are updated regularly to reflect changes in law, healthcare, and best practices, ensuring you always have current guidance.

About the Cover Art

The cover of *Clarity Before Crisis* visually reflects the book's mission. The open hands embody care, protection, and guidance, a reminder of the support we extend to our loved ones as we prepare for the future.

At the center rests a heart, symbolizing family, compassion, and legacy, the values that tie together every decision we make.

Within the heart are three icons, each representing a pillar of preparedness: a piggy bank for financial stability, a gavel for legal authority and planning, and a stethoscope for health and medical care. Together, these elements capture the holistic approach of the book: <u>true readiness requires attention to every area of life.</u>

The design conveys a sense of peace, strength, and confidence. It illustrates that by taking thoughtful steps before a crisis, we not only safeguard our own future but also offer our families the lasting gift of security and reassurance.

Acknowledgements

This book would not have been possible without the support of many people who shaped both the work itself and the journey behind it:

1. My clients: Thank you for entrusting me with your financial well-being, your families, and your futures. It is an honor and a privilege to serve you.

2. My employer: Authoring a book while leading a financial planning practice was no small task. Your trust and support gave me the space to bring this project to life.

3. My firm: Ensuring this work was both powerful and compliant was a challenge. Thank you for walking with me through the details and making publication possible.

4. Marty Bodnar: Your estate planning expertise and ability to translate the complex into the simple have been a gift. You helped me avoid the weeds and focus on conciseness.

5. Joanne Giardini-Russell: Your guidance and insights in the Medicare chapter were invaluable.

6. My loved ones: Thank you for allowing me to share our family stories in ways that honored and dignified the innocent. I hope that these pages bring healing.

7. My wife and children: Time is our most precious asset, and creating this book required much of it. Thank you for believing in me and for giving me the space to pursue this work.

Disclaimers

Tax & Legal Disclaimer

The examples and strategies in this book are provided for educational purposes only and do not constitute legal or tax advice. Laws, regulations, and interpretations change frequently. Readers should consult a qualified professional for guidance specific to their situation.

Healthcare / Medicare Disclaimer

Medicare premiums, deductibles, and program rules change annually. Any figures or thresholds mentioned are subject to adjustment by the Centers for Medicare & Medicaid Services (CMS). Always review the most recent Medicare publications or speak with a licensed healthcare professional before making decisions.

General "timestamp" reminder

This book reflects information available as of 2025. Updates may have occurred since that time. For example, the One Big Beautiful Bill was passed this year, but has not fully gone into effect as of this writing.

Audience

This book is for families and the individuals serving alongside them, because planning for aging, caregiving, and legacy is never just an individual issue. It impacts spouses, children, and future generations.

- **Spouses and Partners**
  You are often the first to face the realities of illness, incapacity, or loss. Planning ahead protects not only your financial stability, but also your relationship and peace of mind.
- **Adult Children**
  Many of you have already lived through caregiving for a parent. It may feel "too late" to plan for them, but it is not too early to plan for yourself. You now carry the lessons, and sometimes the scars, of what happens when planning was incomplete. This book will help you prepare differently for your own future and your children's.
- **Families Together**
  The most powerful planning happens in conversation, not isolation. Whether you are a spouse, child, sibling, or caregiver, the tools in these chapters are designed to bring families together, reduce conflict, and create conviction about what comes next.

Planning is not just for "the wealthy" or for "later." It is for anyone who wants to protect what matters most: your time, health, relationships, and legacy.

A Note to Financial Professionals, Attorneys, and Care Advocates

If you're a financial advisor, estate attorney, care manager, or any other professional serving aging families, this book was written with you in mind, too.

You already know the truth: there's no single plan, person, or product that can meet all the needs of a family facing aging, caregiving, and legacy decisions. It takes a compassionate team of professionals who are willing to go beyond the technical and engage with the human side of planning.

Clarity Before Crisis was never meant to be a marketing piece for my firm. I don't see myself as competition, but as part of the solution. It was created to initiate more meaningful conversations, raise awareness, and provide a practical guide that can help families and the professionals who serve them navigate aging with resolve, purpose, and confidence.

If you're already guiding families through these transitions, this book can serve as a valuable tool in your process:

- A resource for adult children facing sudden caregiving decisions
- A conversation starter for clients delaying estate planning conversations
- A value-add for workshops, review meetings, or community education events
- A framework for integrating financial, legal, and healthcare planning

If you are a:

- **Financial Planner or Advisor**: Use this book to uncover emotional and logistical gaps in your client's current plan. Offer to share this with their beneficiaries and trusted contacts.
- **Attorney**: Pair this guide with your estate documents to help clients communicate intentions beyond the legal language. Provide it to the beneficiaries, executors, or persons named in the Power of Attorney.
- **Care Manager, Clergy, Life Coach, or Social Worker**: Share it with families as they navigate complex transitions, especially when family roles are unclear.
- **Tax Professional or CPA**: Help clients understand how their long-term care, gifting, or inheritance plans intersect with tax strategy.

A Note to the DIY Reader

If you've received this book and are thinking, "I can do most of this myself", you probably can, at least some of it. In fact, the book and website were created to give you a lot of what you need.

Here's my encouragement: don't go it alone.

Whether it's a Certified Financial Planner™, elder law attorney, Medicaid specialist, or care manager, there are professionals who do this every day and know where plans most often fall apart.

Ask for help. It's not weakness, it's wisdom.

The stakes are too high to rely on guesswork. Even if you're confident in your plan, a second set of eyes can provide assurance, catch minor errors, or offer insight you hadn't considered.

Foreword

It was a typical Tuesday in the office. The room was clean and minimal, designed to be orderly and professional. Most people came in to discuss the markets, review portfolios, or ask how to invest under the current administration. I usually had four of these meetings a day. Then I met Diane.

She sat across from me with tears running down her face, the kind of tears that come only after years of holding everything together. Diane had just returned to Michigan after several years in Florida, where she had left her husband and teenage children behind in order to care for her aging father. She had carried the weight of sibling conflict through his health crises. She had endured a long and painful probate battle. And now, with her father gone, she found herself entering an entirely new phase of life.

I asked her if she had allowed herself time to grieve. She shook her head. *"No. How could I? I was still a mom. I was still a wife. I was still managing everything."*

Her words broke my heart because they revealed both her strength and her exhaustion. Beneath all the responsibility, she was still someone's daughter.

When we finally turned the conversation toward her own future, she spoke quietly about her hopes. She wanted to get back on track for retirement, make sure she would never become a burden on her children, and age with dignity herself.

Real life, like Diane's, isn't a clean office environment. It is messy, unpredictable, and resistant to textbook answers.

That conversation marked me. At the time, I did not have every tool or resource I wished I could offer her. What I did have was the conviction that families like Diane's deserved more. Her story became the spark that lit this work: the realization that caregiving, conflict, finances, and legacy are not separate issues. They collide, and if families are not prepared, the cost is devastating.

The Rising Wave

Diane's story is deeply personal, yet it is not unique. What happened in her family is already unfolding in living rooms, courtrooms, and hospital corridors across the country. Her tears were a warning sign of something larger rising beneath the surface, a generational wave often called the *Silver Tsunami.*

Do you understand how a tsunami begins?
It does not form with storm clouds gathering on the horizon. Storms can be tracked; warnings can be issued. A tsunami begins deep beneath the surface with an earthquake no one can predict. Silent. Sudden. Invisible until it rises.

The devastation of a tsunami is well known. We also know one is coming. What remains uncertain is how or when it will strike your family.

Consider the glaring fault lines we're seeing now:

- **$72 trillion** will transfer between generations in the next 20 years (Investments & Wealth Institute).
- **67%** of Americans have no estate plan (CNBC).
- The American Health Care Association and National Center for Assisted Living says "access to care is a national crisis". They cite closings, labor shortages, development costs, max occupancy, and waiting lists as concerns they hope to address.

- McKinsey and Company projects a shortage of 100,000 wealth advisors by 2034.
- It is estimated there are **53 million** unpaid caregivers in the United States.

I could go on, but you get the picture. The wave is rising. The institutions we have relied upon are straining. The window for proactive planning grows narrower each year. The government isn't coming to save you. Many of the professionals you've relied on are facing it themselves. The burden rests on you.

To the caregiver, especially: I wrote this with you in mind. I hope you feel welcomed, understood, and supported. Within these pages, you will find an ally who has sat with families like yours, listened to their struggles, and fought for their victories.

The Hard Truths

This is not the censored, carefully curated message you may hear at a seminar or read in a glossy brochure. This is the conversation behind closed doors, at the kitchen table, in the middle of real human emotion.

Here you will encounter the truths most people avoid:

- The midnight calls that change everything.
- The family fractures that money cannot mend.
- The fatigue of caregiving.
- The cost of postponing difficult conversations.

You cannot avoid hard conversations. These are some of the most difficult you'll have because you're facing trauma, grief, illness, and death. With that, you have two options: Hard now or hard later. Pay now or potentially pay more later. If there is

anything I've learned, hard later is worse, much worse, and more expensive.

Here is the deeper truth: families do not fail because they do not care. They fail because no one shows them how to prepare. Without guidance, they postpone conversations, avoid decisions, and hope tomorrow will be easier. Tomorrow often brings the midnight phone call, the diagnosis, the sudden confrontation.

The greatest danger isn't just running out of money. It's running out of time.

It's time to have difficult conversations, get organized, and prepare before life delivers the unexpected.

My Why

My own life hasn't been a bed of roses, either. They say those who've experienced trauma can be the best at guiding others through it. When I was eight, my father died of cancer. I did not grasp the details, but I lived the grief, the confusion, and the aftermath. It took decades to process that loss, and it impressed on me the fragility of life and the urgency of time.

Years later, as an Army officer, I witnessed loss again, through combat and through suicide. In that world, preparation was not optional; it was survival. We drilled transitions and contingencies relentlessly because lives depended on it. The words we carried still echo: *"Standards, no compromise. Proffer no excuses. Forward ever, backward never."* Clarity was the standard. Crisis was the cost of neglect.

I have also seen the same struggles in my own extended family as caregiving and end-of-life decisions arose. Even when money and documents were present, the lack of communication and coordination left loved ones derailed.

That conviction led me to pursue the CFP® designation, to work for a firm that allowed me to serve clients independently, and to author this book.

A Different Kind of Writer

I am not a journalist collecting stories. I admire writers like Malcolm Gladwell who make complex issues accessible through story, yet my work comes from a different place.

I am not an academic advancing theory, though I deeply respect the role of research and higher education in shaping this field. My office sits just down the road from the University of Michigan, a constant reminder of the value of rigorous study and the pursuit of knowledge.

This book is not written to impress or entertain. It is written to prepare you and those you love for the moments that matter most.

I am a practitioner. Each week, I sit with families facing these very challenges. I work alongside attorneys drafting documents, tax planners organizing returns, and caregivers carrying burdens that few people ever see.

Separate from the Pack

If you found this book among the countless titles on personal finance and retirement, this one takes a different approach. While many works fall into the common categories of money, tax, and estate planning, or finding purpose, each leaves something unaddressed. Real life does not occur in silos. When aging, caregiving, or loss arrives, every sphere collides at once: health, money, family, documents, and legacy. If these areas are not connected, even the most carefully prepared plan can unravel.

This book integrates these disciplines into a single, practical guide, designed not only to be read but to be used, so that you can **prepare in advance** and **lead your family with confidence**.

Inside, you will learn how to:

- **Prioritize** decisions before a crisis limits your choices.
- **Avoid** common pitfalls that create financial and emotional strain.
- **Engage** the right professionals at the right time, with clear understanding of their available strategies.
- **Build** a plan that protects health, wealth, and relationships, ensuring that your family is supported and your legacy endures.

This is not merely a financial planning book. It is a life planning book, one that weaves together dollars, documents, health, and family into a resilient strategy.

Not Only for the "Wealthy"

Too often, people assume financial planning is only for the wealthy or the sophisticated, the people with large portfolios, complex estates, or business empires. That's simply not true.

Yes, wealthy families may benefit from advanced strategies in investing, taxes, and estate planning. The heart of this book is not about complexity; it's about clarity.

<u>A plan isn't a luxury for the wealthy; it's a necessity for everyone.</u>

Whether you're caring for aging parents, preparing for retirement on a modest income, or simply trying to protect the people you love, having a plan in place can mean the difference between calm and chaos.

Planning is not about the size of your bank account. It's about aligning your financial, emotional, relational, and even spiritual resources with the life you want to live. I call it harmony between life and money. You don't need millions to benefit from clarity. You just need the willingness to think ahead and take simple, intentional steps.

That's why this book exists: to help families of all kinds face the future with confidence.

The Vision of What Is Possible

When these ideas are put into practice, I believe something amazing can happen.

Families can thrive across generations, not only financially but emotionally, relationally, and spiritually. Legacies can be built, strengthened, and protected so that future generations inherit more than wealth. They can inherit values, stories, and enduring connection.

Memories can be passed down and celebrated so that the lives of those who came before will continue to inspire those who follow.

Business owners and retirees can enter the next stage of life with confidence, peace, and hope, so that their years of work are crowned with rest rather than conflict or fear.

Wealth can be passed down across families without division or resentment, so that unity rather than discord defines the transfer.

Giving and generosity can expand so that families not only safeguard their own, but also strengthen their communities and the causes they cherish.

Achieving this requires a different approach. Planning must extend beyond spreadsheets, wills, and insurance policies. It must create clarity that connects money to meaning, documents to values, and wealth to legacy. This book exists to help families choose clarity before crisis.

An Inside Look

Throughout this book, you'll be introduced to a number of people. You'll get a peek at their stories and families. My desire is that you see yourself in them. Let their voices in the pages ahead inspire you, teach you, and guide you.

You'll hear about the son who opened his home to his mother and the daughter who oversaw the care of both parents.

You'll meet a widow and a widower, as well as some business owners, and then see how their mark was left on the world.

A Final Word

Crisis emerges when clarity is absent. It is the midnight phone call, the diagnosis, the sudden confrontation. Crisis leaves families scrambling, siblings in conflict, and decision-making resting on the shoulders of the least prepared. It strips away options, peace of mind, and often even relationships. Once it arrives, there is no chance to turn back.

Clarity is what steadies a person when the ground begins to shift. It does not eliminate life's storms, yet it allows us to face them with open eyes, calm confidence, and purposeful action. Clarity brings freedom: the freedom to focus on health, relationships, and meaning, knowing the essentials are already in place.

As you read the clarity affirmations at the end of each chapter, you'll feel yourself gaining it. Stand on the shores with confidence because you've found your harbor in the storm.

Welcome. Let us begin.

Part 1: Building the Foundation

CHAPTER ONE

Laying the Foundation: A House Built on the Rock

"It's not how old you are, but how you are old."

Jules Renard

When it comes to building a truly wealthy life, age matters far less than clarity. The most resilient, confident retirees I've met didn't just have money; they identified what mattered most to them *before* life threw them a curveball.

Your planning journey unfolds in three major phases:

- **Accumulation**
- **Retirement Preparation**
- **Retirement.**

Each brings unique choices, challenges, and opportunities to shape the life you want. This chapter is where it begins, not with numbers, but with clarity. Think of it as your launch point for protecting what matters most, long before life throws its curveballs.

If you take away one idea from this chapter, it's this: the greatest planning tool you have is your voice. Communication skills are the key. Communicating your beliefs, values, goals, dreams, and concerns is the key differentiator.

On Planning

I'm a planner. It's part of my DNA at this point, though it wasn't always like that. I was more of a go-with-the-flow type as a youth. That changed when I joined the Army as a reconnaissance scout.

I learned tactics, strategy, and how to prepare for multiple possible futures. Observation and communication were our primary tools and owning the outcome was a key point of emphasis. In guerrilla warfare and counterinsurgency, you are constantly navigating the gray area. Later, as an officer, I was part of current ops and future ops, AKA near-term and long-term planning.

Oddly enough, preparing for retirement, or for a long life well-lived, can be more complex than deploying a quick reaction force. In life, there's no formal briefing before the next challenge arrives.

I've lived through the unexpected:

- Losing my father to cancer
- A miscarriage with my wife
- Career-altering musculoskeletal tears in my foot and knee
- A detour from my plan to work on Wall Street into personal financial planning (a change I'm now deeply grateful for)

The military also taught me to find the smallest light at the end of the tunnel, to be resilient, and to have hope against insurmountable obstacles and odds.

You can't predict every crisis, but you can be ready for them.

If you're reading this and thinking, *Life hasn't gone according to plan for me either*, **you're not alone**. You might have retired earlier than expected, faced health challenges, or been thrown into caregiving without warning. Life is dynamic, so it doesn't care about your spreadsheet. Even if your past wasn't planned, your future *can* be.

2 Challenges of Traditional Financial Planning

Traditional planning often jumps straight into numbers and products, ignoring the foundation of values and life clarity. That's why so many people feel underserved or misunderstood. Here are two of the biggest gaps I see in traditional planning…

Challenge 1: The Script Is Not Written in Stone

For much of our lives, we're told to follow a script, whether we realize it or not:

Go to college.
Get a job.
Get married.
Buy a house.
Have kids.
Raise them well.
Then… retire.

If you've chosen a different path, you might feel like a rebel, a maverick, or a trailblazer, someone going against the grain. Perhaps your family questioned your choices or gave you a hard time for not following the traditional script. Their concerns likely stemmed from a place of love, with a desire to see you safe, accepted, and secure in the world, even though many of the happiest and most fulfilled people I know took a different path.

Why Do So Many Advisors Stick to the Textbook?

Suppose we know that deviating from the standard path can lead to incredible success and self-fulfillment. Then why do so many traditional advisors stick to the textbook and traditional advice?

They do this because it's safe, familiar, and compliant. It's what they were taught to do. Most advisors are trained to follow a linear process: projecting retirement income, recommending products, and checking boxes. You'll see why that approach so often fails.

It doesn't mean they're a bad advisor, so let's be clear on that. It means the total financial world is nuanced and complex. Many advisors serve more families than they can reasonably handle. Some are limited by the goals of their firm.

If your advisor isn't talking to you about these topics, don't be surprised. They may never bring it up on their own. At the end of the day, you need to advocate for yourself and your family. The same advisor who helped you get to retirement may not be the best one to help you see it through. If that's the case, start exploring advisors who can help you pursue your goals now.

Challenge 2: Retirement Is Not the End of the Plan

We're told that retirement is the goal. It's the final milestone, the reward, and the finish line. Depending on who you are, that's either glamorous or terrifying. What if it's not the end at all? What if it's the beginning of an entirely new phase of life?

If traditional planning falls short, what does work? The answer lies in pairing lived experience with structure.

Experience Matters, But So Does Structure

Maybe you're a mature adult with tons of life experience. You've seen things textbooks don't cover. You've lived through market crashes, divorce, child raising, job losses, caregiving, and real-life messiness. That kind of wisdom matters. Experience teaches lessons the hard way, but planning helps you avoid learning them twice.

You might be thinking, "I've lived a long life. I've seen what happens. I don't need a fancy plan."

You're right; your experience matters. You've gained insight the hard way, and that wisdom should shape your future.

What if we paired your lived experience with tools that prevent regret, protect the people you love, and give you more freedom, not less?

Planning isn't about control; it's about *clarity*. It's not punishment; it's *the possibility of freedom*. Neither is it perfection; it's *preparedness*.

You may not think of yourself as a planner, but you already are. We all plan, but for varied reasons.

Type of Planning	Description
Plan to Achieve	You're focused on goals. You want to retire early, buy a lake house, or leave a legacy. You plan to win.
Plan to Prevent	You've seen what happens when there's no plan: family conflict, financial ruin, unnecessary stress. You plan to avoid pain.
Plan to Recover	You've lived through loss, illness, or unexpected change. You know life can unravel fast. You plan to get back on your feet. You may not have had the chance to prepare for what happened, but you can plan for what's next. What kind of life would bring you peace, even now?
Plan to Move Forward	You're stuck. You don't want to be, but you don't know what's next. Planning helps you get unstuck and regain direction. Even if you're late to start, it's not too late to begin.
Plan to Maximize	You're doing well, and you want to do better. Planning helps you make the most of your time, energy, money, and relationships.

A Different Approach

As an advisor, I've taken numerous classes and passed many exams.

- State life, accident, and health insurance
- Variable products and annuities
- *Series 7 General Securities Representative Qualification Exam
- *Series 66 Uniform Combined State Law Examination
- CFP® Board Exam

*Licenses held with LPL Financial

Additionally, I've dedicated extra hours to continuing education, product training, industry-recommended books, newsletters, and market briefings.

Through all of that, I've learned the textbook, so I'm not some self-made guru fighting the system. I have developed the judgment to know when the textbook applies and when real life requires something more.

My Planning Philosophy

Planning, to me, is not about predicting the future; it's about preparing for it. It's not rigid control; it's resilience. My approach blends tactical discipline from my military background with the holistic, human-centered framework of financial life planning. It's about aligning money with meaning, structure with flexibility, and strategy with the values that make life worth living.

Psychology

My approach may seem unconventional because it aims to address history, behaviors, mindsets, and personal scripts. These may be uncomfortable to address. Even the CFP Board now requires

Psychology of Financial Planning education, because they've seen real change and progress happen in our minds before it is reflected on paper. *Psychology of Money* by Morgan Housel is immensely helpful in this space, along with *Start Thinking Rich* by Dr. Brad Klontz and Adrian Brambila. *Mind Over Money Management* by Robyn Craine also goes deep into our mental scripts and personal history to explore our attitudes about money that can hold us back.

The Planning Pyramid

Imagine a pyramid. At the base are your values, beliefs, and vision, which serve as the foundation. Above that are your relationships, health, and independence. Once those layers are stable, adding the financial tools: investments, tax planning, estate planning, and insurance has an even greater impact. At the top sits wealth transfer and legacy.

Too often, people flip the pyramid upside down by starting with products, investments, or tax tricks, but without prioritizing what truly matters. That creates instability, as changes in life or the market can make a house of cards come crashing down. My approach builds from the bottom up. While others may stop planning once they've achieved retirement or financial independence, we take it a step further to build family unity and create a lasting legacy.

Once the foundation is clear, structure comes from a proven planning process, which provides a disciplined yet flexible way to carry that clarity forward.

The 7-Step Planning Process

To bring this philosophy into practice, I follow a 7-step process:

1. **Understand** your **personal and financial** circumstances. This isn't just financial statements, but your story.
2. **Identify** practical and aspirational goals.

3. **Analyze** your current course. What's working? What's not?
4. **Develop** recommendations. Because I understand you deeply and what you want to achieve, I provide tailored strategies, not cookie-cutter advice.
5. **Present** clearly. This is about translating complexity into clarity.
6. **Implemen**t together. Action beats theory, and it's why I emphasize the importance of collaboration and a planning team.
7. **Review** and adapt. Life changes; your plan must too.

This process ensures structure without rigidity, accountability without pressure, and understanding without jargon.

My clients hire me to provide them with direct guidance, as they come to me seeking clarity. As you're reading this, my role isn't to tell you what to do. It's to make sure your values and experience are reflected in a plan that works when life throws its curveballs.

A Modern Approach

Life doesn't happen in straight lines; it happens in swerves. Real planning means addressing the *orange-to-yellow* shift: the moment your predictable path turns into real-world unpredictability. This higher level of planning requires nuance, empathy, and the willingness to challenge a system that often prioritizes efficiency over humanity.

From this nuance, I created a life planning timeline that I use in my process (below). It maps out key life milestones and brings the entire planning journey into focus. The orange section reflects the traditional, rules-based path. This is the one many people expect to follow. The yellow section is where things get real. It represents the detours, disruptions, and unexpected turns that often shape our lives.

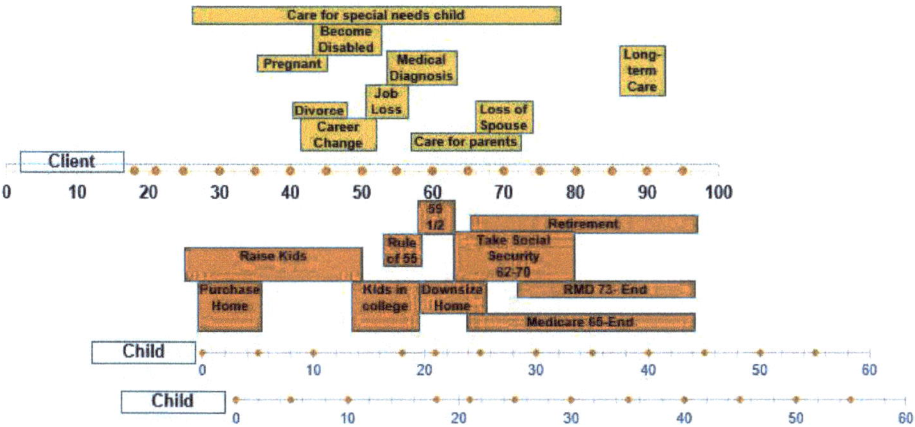

Those moments, such as the diagnosis, the divorce, and the call from the memory care home, are the moments that can break even the most well-designed plan. Good things can change the plan too, such as early retirement, getting remarried, or a life-changing inheritance.

While financial planning software can calculate things like tax brackets, inflation, income growth, and life expectancy, real planning goes beyond the math. That's why I don't just build projections, I run scenarios. Life rarely follows the script.

Let's Rethink Retirement

Retirement isn't about what's ending, but what's beginning. It's your opportunity to design a life centered on meaning rather than obligation. You could rediscover parts of yourself that were buried under decades of doing what needed to be done. You could invest in relationships, passions, health, and purpose, not because you have to, but because you finally can.

The structure that you relied on and helped you (or harmed you, as we'll see shortly) through your working years may not serve you in retirement. You'll need a new one, one you build intentionally.

Vision First

"What's your vision for the future?" When I first meet with someone nearing that "finish line," I ask that simple opening question that sets the tone for the rest of our planning conversations. The answer I'm looking for is anything but simple. Many people are financially ready, characterized by low debt, healthy savings, and a solid cash flow. But when I ask if they want to prioritize lifestyle or legacy, they go silent. The most common response? ***"I don't know. I've never thought about it."***

That always stops me in my tracks. You've spent 30 or 40 years working hard, saving diligently, sacrificing for your family, and you've never thought about *what it was all for?*

Most people want "enough." But when I ask, "Enough for what?" they're unsure.

That's when we start digging.

- Do you want to relocate to a warmer place, maybe buy a beach house?
- Do you want to travel the world or visit the grandkids more often?
- Should we create a giving strategy for causes or people you care about?
- Do you want to buy a boat? An RV? A motorcycle?

Emotional Wealth: Planning Beyond the Numbers

James Clear, in his bestselling book, *Atomic Habits*, explains how deeply our behaviors are tied to our identity and past experiences.

Many people enter retirement carrying more than just a financial portfolio; they bring emotional scars, past traumas, and limiting beliefs.

- If you've lost a job or lived through a major market crash, fear may drive your financial decisions.
- If you've worked hard to climb out of debt or strictly save, you may feel allergic to spending even when you can afford it.
- If you've been betrayed or hurt in relationships, trust may be hard to rebuild, even with professionals.
- If you weren't in a season where travel or generosity was possible, it may feel unfamiliar at first.

The harsh truth: Most people can't just flip the switch

That fear can become a lifestyle. Success becomes not *thriving*, but simply *not losing everything*. Retirement shouldn't be about just surviving. It can be about living intentionally and abundantly.

Habits shape us, but they can also evolve.

When planning for the future, it can be challenging to achieve a clear perspective. It's unclear because our past and present can cloud our understanding. A couple in their late 50s struggled to think big because they were consumed with getting their kids through college first. If you saw a loved one die young, you may not be ecstatic about your work-free future.

Two Types of Retirees

60 going on 90

Stop working and stop living. Health declines and quality of life drops quickly. Your career was your entire identity; now you're aimless without it. You gave it everything, won the race, and came to an empty finish line.

70 going on 40

Age is a number, and you feel much younger than you may look. Your calendar is complete as you spend time with the friends, family, and community you've built. Your health is a foundation for a long and enjoyable life.

It's important to recognize that "60 going on 90" doesn't just describe someone who failed to plan. I often meet incredibly successful, accomplished people who fall into this category.

The High Achiever: You spent decades building a business or rising through the ranks of your profession. You were respected, admired, and at the top of your game. But when you stop working, that well-defined sense of self disappears. Without the meetings, the goals, the titles, or the team, you feel lost. That energy that once filled the room fades. You were able to burn the candle at both ends, and now your health declines. You may be quietly grieving the life left behind.

On the flip side, I've also seen people who disliked their job for years. Some even hated it, but kept going because it gave them structure, a community, or a reason to get out of bed. Work was the only thing anchoring their day. When it's gone, there's a void they never anticipated.

Both types struggle, not because they lack money, but because they lack purpose. Retirement doesn't automatically fill that gap.

As you think about the types of retirees, I'm sure you can see yourself in one of them easily. You can also think of people you know who fit the other type as well. If you're unsure, here are some questions to gain deeper insight:

1. What do I do for fun?

2. Do I have hobbies, passions, or a community?
3. Who am I when I'm not working?
4. Do I spend my time and energy *on* others, or just *on* myself?
5. Is my calendar full of meaningful activity, or is it mostly empty and full of obligatory events?
6. What's my vision for retirement?
7. How do I want to be remembered?
8. Is my outlook on life hopeful and purpose-driven, or does it depend on the news, the market, or the next substantial change?

These answers reveal everything about your identity beyond your job, title, or bank account.

Planning for retirement isn't just about the numbers; it's about knowing *who you are* and *what you want.*

You may be reading and saying to yourself, "I'd like to think I have a good vision for retirement, and that I'll be around to enjoy it. I may not have answers to all those questions yet, but I'll figure it out."

While it's tempting to assume everything will fall into place, experience tells us otherwise. Retirement requires intention.

The fundamental difference between a retiree who thrives and one who declines isn't found in their bank account; it's in their sense of identity, purpose, and connection. It's not just how much you've saved, but how well you've prepared to live.

You've heard that sentiment before, and you may believe it. That may sound good or feel good but typically doesn't translate to meaningful change.

To address this challenge, I created the **Legacy Wealth Scorecard**. It's easy to measure our income and net worth, but it's difficult to assess the qualitative factors of our lives. My assessment gives you a practical way to measure what matters: the quality of your time, your health, your relationships, and your independence. The assessment is subjective, but targets specific attitudes and behaviors, rather than broad ideas.

True Wealth =

Financial and time independence +

Physical health +

Emotional & spiritual well-being +

Relationships

When you answer those questions honestly, you'll start to see where you are strong and where you might need to grow. You can download it for free online. Give yourself a baseline, then reassess over time to track progress.

It Starts Earlier Than You Think

One of the most common misconceptions about retirement is that everything will magically fall into place once you leave your job.

It doesn't.

People who enjoy retirement the most, who thrive in it, are the ones who *started living like retirees before they retired.* They built habits, communities, routines, and self-awareness while they were still in the accumulation or preparation phase. They didn't wait until they had "more time." They planted the tree years ago so that they could sit in the shade today.

Maybe you wish you'd started earlier. That's okay. The second-best time to begin is today. No matter what stage you're in, now is the time to start thinking deeply about the life you want and the steps to get there.

Clarity Affirmations

- Now I know preparation creates freedom, not restriction.
- I can picture the life I want, not just the one I fear.
- I understand why planning early gives my family peace.
- I will take the first step toward clarity before crisis.

Action Plan

1. **Reflect.**
   Write down your vision for retirement. What does an enjoyable day look like? A wonderful year?
2. **Clarify identity.**
   List who you are outside of work. What roles do you play? What brings you purpose?
3. **Identify joy.**
   Name three things you'd enjoy doing if you had more time.
4. **Take stock of your wealth equation with the Legacy Wealth Scorecard.**
   Give yourself a simple rating in three areas:

   - Independence and freedom (time + money)
   - Health (physical, emotional, spiritual)
   - Relationships (family, community, contribution)

Other thought leaders, like Sahil Bloom, have broadened the conversation with *The 5 Types of Wealth*. He discusses financial, social, time, physical, and mental. This framework is a powerful reminder that true wealth is bigger than money.

My wealth equation complements that perspective. Where his model inspires us to reimagine wealth, mine gives you a way to measure it in daily life. It's simple, direct, and trackable: a tool to help you turn inspiration into action and see your progress over time.

Ramit Sethi's book *I Will Teach You to Be Rich* is another helpful resource as he helps readers define their "rich life." The premise of the book is that you define your own American Dream, rather than getting caught up in comparisons. It's not about how much money you make, but how much you keep and what you allocate it to.

- **Assess your time.**
  Look at your calendar. Are you spending time on what matters most?
- **Start living it now.**
  Pick one "retirement habit" to try this month: join a community, pick up a hobby, or take a small trip. Don't wait.

Looking Ahead

In the next chapter, we'll look closely at the **Accumulation Phase,** where it all begins, and how setting the proper foundation early leads to true wealth later.

CHAPTER TWO
The Accumulation Phase: Building on the Foundation

"A good plan today is better than a perfect plan tomorrow."

George S. Patton

When you're in your 20s, 30s, 40s, and even early 50s, the future can feel like a far-off destination. Retirement, caregiving, and legacy planning seem like something for "later." The problem is, later has a way of arriving suddenly—sometimes with little warning. That's when people find themselves in crisis mode, scrambling to make decisions with limited options.

The accumulation phase of earning, saving, and building is where *clarity before crisis* matters most. It's when you lay the groundwork for financial security, resilience, and the freedom to make choices on your own terms.

Clarity Matters Early

Too many people drift through the accumulation years on autopilot. They save a little, invest here and there, maybe contribute to a 401(k), but without a clear, intentional plan. The problem isn't just that they might not save enough; it's that they miss the chance to build flexibility into their future.

When clarity is missing, people often:

- Overcommit to debt and limit future freedom.
- Delay important insurance and legal protections until it's too late.

- Neglect to invest in relationships, health, and skills that will matter more than money in later years.

But when clarity is present, each decision about spending, saving, career changes, or major purchases lines up with a bigger vision. You're not just growing your accounts; you're growing the life you want to live.

Let's start with what this phase often looks like through the lens of two real people.

Two Paths: Tom and Karen

Tom's Story: The Cost of Drifting Without Clarity

Tom, a mid-40s engineer, made a great income and consistently maxed out his retirement accounts. On paper, he was doing everything right, but when we met, he admitted he had no real vision for the next 10–15 years. His plan was essentially: "Keep working until I can't."

His schedule left no room for personal growth, hobbies, or even rest. His marriage was strained, not from conflict, but from neglect. These were years of putting work first and assuming there would be "time later" to focus on each other.

When his company underwent a sudden downsizing, Tom found himself unemployed, emotionally strained, and questioning everything. His finances could weather the storm, but emotionally and relationally, he was unprepared.

Tom's problem wasn't a lack of work ethic, but a lack of clarity. He had delayed making the investments in his life that money couldn't fix.

Karen's Story: What Preparation Looks Like

Karen, also in her 40s, approached accumulation differently. She still worked hard, but she took her PTO every year, even if it meant a "staycation" with her family. She and her husband had a weekly date night. She set aside time for things she loved, like gardening, even during busy seasons at work.

Financially, she contributed to her retirement plan, but she also invested in personal development. She took leadership courses, worked with a mentor, and built a strong professional network. She also made her health a priority with regular exercise and preventive care.

When Karen's father was diagnosed with dementia, she was able to adjust her work schedule, lean on her network, and step into a caregiving role without her life unraveling. She didn't just have savings; she had the emotional and relational capacity to navigate the unexpected.

The Little Lies We Tell Ourselves

Tom and Karen's stories aren't just about decisions-they're about the *stories we tell ourselves.*

Most people don't plan to neglect their marriage, health, or joy. They simply believe a few **"little lies"** that push intentional living into a vague "later" that may never come.

We all have them, those small, quiet phrases we repeat in our minds that make us feel better about putting things off. They aren't malicious or dramatic, but over time, they create a dangerous gap between what we *say* we want and how we actually live.

Here are a few of the most common:

- I'll take that trip when work slows down.
- We'll have more time for date nights once the kids are older.
- I'll start that hobby after I retire.
- I'll get in shape when life isn't so hectic.

- I'll work on personal growth later. Right now, I just need to grind.

The truth?
Life rarely "slows down" on its own. On the contrary, it's often because of circumstances you didn't choose: job loss, illness, or other unexpected changes.

Why These Lies Are So Believable

They sound harmless, maybe even wise. Nobody questions you when you say, "We'll get to that later." In fact, most people nod in agreement because they're telling themselves the same thing. Busyness has become a socially acceptable badge of honor, something to brag about over another cup of coffee or glass of wine to keep up the pace. But "later" is slippery because it keeps moving. For some, it never comes at all.

What Happens Instead

- PTO days expire unused.
- Skills you meant to learn never get started.
- Friendships and marriages quietly drift apart.
- Your health and energy aren't what they used to be. The extra pregnancy weight and dad bod become permanent fixtures.
- You wake up one day and realize the window for that dream you were saving has already closed.

The Alternative: Live It Now, in Small Ways

You don't have to quit your job and move to the beach. But you *can*:

- Use the vacation days you've been hoarding.
- Plan a date night this month, even if it's just takeout and a walk.

- Sign up for that class or start that hobby now, before you "have time."
- Invest in your health and personal development like it's a retirement account, knowing small, steady contributions pay off.

Money Mindsets

Our relationship with money is shaped less by numbers and more by mindset. Two of the most powerful forces are **greed** and **fear.**

Greed: The Internal Voice

Greed doesn't always look like extravagance. It often sounds like subtle whispers of comparison or entitlement:

- *"Once I make X, I'll finally be happy."*
- *"Must be nice to have what they have."*
- *"It's not fair that they get ahead while I struggle."*
- *"They can figure it out themselves. I need to look out for me."*
- *"I'd be better off if I just had…"*

Greed keeps us chasing satisfaction that never arrives. It tricks us into believing joy lies just one step, one purchase, or one dollar amount away.

Fear: The External Voice

Fear is the flip side of the coin. It often comes from outside influences, magnified by headlines, social media, and economic noise:

- *"Who knows what'll happen tomorrow?"*
- *"I can't afford to take that risk."*
- *"Did you hear the news? Things are getting worse."*

- *"I read on Facebook that the market is crashing."*
- *"Did you see the price of gas? Groceries? Everything's going up."*
- *"I'm going to wait until things settle down."*

Fear keeps us paralyzed, hesitant to act, always waiting for the "right time."

Money and Marriage: The Financial Dynamics

Money in marriage can either unite or divide. Many couples stumble when one spouse carries all the responsibility, or when finances are hidden. Others thrive by keeping money decisions transparent and shared.

The Risks of Separation:

- One spouse controls the money while the other is left in the dark.
- Accounts are kept separate or hidden.
- Financial decisions exclude the other spouse.
- Lack of insurance, emergency savings, or estate planning leaves the family vulnerable.

The Rewards of Partnership:

- Joint accounts foster openness and accountability.
- Regular family meetings set shared goals.
- Couples celebrate progress — like paying down debt, saving for travel, or planning retirement.
- Big decisions, such as updating the house or funding kids' education, are made together.

- Protections are put in place: POA, will, trust, and adequate insurance.

Money in marriage isn't just about numbers. It's about trust, transparency, and teamwork.

Key Financial Areas of Focus

You're investing in your health, relationships, interests, so now it's time to ensure your finances give you the foundation to build upon.

1. Cash Flow and Debt Management

Your income is your most powerful wealth-building tool during these years. Clarity here means knowing exactly where your money goes, keeping lifestyle inflation in check, and avoiding debt that limits your future flexibility.

2. Emergency Reserves

Aim for at least 3–6 months of expenses, more if you're self-employed or in a volatile industry. This isn't just for peace of mind; it gives you time to make thoughtful decisions instead of desperate ones when something happens.

3. Insurance Protection

Life, disability, and health coverage are foundational. Without them, a single event can derail decades of progress.

4. Retirement Accounts

Contribute to the IRS maximum funding amounts for tax-advantaged accounts, when possible, but also build accessible investments outside retirement accounts for flexibility before age 59½.

5. Legal Documents

Even in your 20s and 30s, a simple Will, Power of Attorney, and healthcare directive can save loved ones from confusion and conflict.

6. Skill-Building and Relationships

Financial capital matters, but social and personal capital are equally important. Keep learning, growing your network, and strengthening relationships that will enrich your life later.

Clarity Check: Are You Drifting or Driving?

Ask yourself:

- Do I know my target savings rate? Am I hitting it?
- Could I cover six months of expenses without income?
- Would my family know what to do if something happened to me?
- Am I building skills and relationships that will still matter after I stop working?
- Do I take vacations, or just accumulate unused PTO?

If you're not sure, now is the time to get clear before life makes the decision for you.

In the same way we believe those little lies, we're also taught some of the wrong things about personal finance.

Common Misconceptions

Myth: Don't invest until you're debt-free.
Fact: Not all debt is equal. It may be smarter to invest if your potential returns outpaced your loan interest (e.g., 9% market return vs. 5% debt interest). High-interest debt, such as credit cards, should be prioritized first, but don't ignore investments just because you have a mortgage or student loan.

Myth: Always choose Roth accounts. **Fact:** It depends. If you're in a low tax bracket now, Roth makes sense. If you're in a high bracket, traditional accounts might be better for reducing today's tax burden. Tax strategy is personal, not one-size-fits-all.
Myth: You can't build wealth unless you earn six figures. **Fact:** Wealth is about the gap between income and expenses. Many people earning $40,000 are building wealth. Plenty earning $400K live paycheck to paycheck. Lifestyle choices are more important than income.
Myth: I don't need a Will because I'm not rich. **Fact:** Estate planning isn't about wealth; it's about responsibility. Guardianship for children, Power of Attorney, and medical directives matter at any income level.
Myth: I don't need a CPA or advisor. **Fact:** First, let's differentiate between the two types of tax advisors. Many tax pros are "filers." They look backwards, then input historical data for the current year. The other type is a "planner." They're looking forward. They help you anticipate, strategize, and plan ahead. A CPA focused on tax *planning* (not just filing) can save you far more than their fee. Likewise, a flat-fee financial planner can guide you through life transitions even if you don't have a large portfolio currently.

Clarity Affirmations

- Now I know the foundation I build today shapes my future tomorrow.
- I can see how my habits and choices compound over time.
- I understand that clarity is about direction, not perfection.
- I will commit to small actions that create long-term freedom.

Action Plan

1. **Write down three "little lies"** you've been telling yourself and replace them with specific actions.
2. **Review your financial landscape.** List your debts and investments. What are you paying in interest? What are you earning? Adjust accordingly.
3. **Find a flat-fee planner.** Look for someone aligned with your season of life, whether that's young families, professionals, or small business owners.
4. **Create a simple estate plan.** Consult with an attorney or use a reputable legal service to draft a Will and a POA; review with counsel if possible. If you can follow IKEA instructions, you'll be all right. If IKEA isn't good enough, hire an attorney.
5. **Build community.** Join a group, club, church, or nonprofit. You need relationships that aren't tied to work or your kids' activities.
6. **Start a low-cost hobby now**, something you can see yourself continuing in retirement. If you want something for yourself, that's good, but finding a new community is even better.
7. **Educate yourself.** Read books, listen to podcasts, or take a course on personal finance. Avoid TikTok finance "gurus."

8. **Schedule one recurring activity** that invests in your marriage or closest relationships.

Final Thought

The habits, mindsets, and relationships you cultivate in the accumulation phase will shape your retirement every bit as much as the size of your portfolio. You can't outsource purpose, connection, or health—and you can't assume they'll magically appear once work slows down.

Clarity before crisis means building both your financial foundation and the life you want to live—now. It's using PTO before burnout takes its toll, investing in your marriage before distance creeps in, and starting hobbies before you "have time." It's rejecting the little lies that later will be easier and choosing instead to live in alignment with your values today.

When you carry these habits forward, retirement isn't a cliff you fall off. Instead, it's a continuation of a life you've been living intentionally for years. The groundwork you lay now becomes the launchpad for the next phase: **turning financial stability into freedom, and freedom into fulfillment.** That's where we're headed next.

CHAPTER THREE
Retirement Prep: Final Touch Ups

"Just remember, once you're over the hill, you begin to pick up speed."

Charles Schulz

Ages 50 to 65 signal the retirement preparation phase, a critical window where clarity matters more than ever. Many people shift their focus from building wealth to protecting it, making decisions about income, housing, health care, and legacy. At this stage, the financial questions multiply, but so do the emotional and relational ones.

Earlier in this book, we explored the accumulation phase where habits are formed and vision is clarified. Now, preparation is about taking that clarity and putting it to work **before life changes the rules**. The choices you make here ripple through everything that follows, especially caregiving, estate planning, and family dynamics. You'll see those topics expanded later.

From Child to Caregiver

Mark lay awake in the dark, listening to the rhythmic hiss of the oxygen concentrator down the hall. It had become the soundtrack of his nights. The ceiling glowed faintly with the green digits of the alarm clock, each minute stretching longer than the last. His thoughts refused to quiet: his mother's recovery, his wife's patience, the bills waiting on his desk, the teenagers whose lives had been quietly rearranged around all of it.

At fifty-two, Mark was supposed to be in his stride; married, two kids in high school, a stable management job he could do from home. The arrangement had once felt perfect. He could make breakfast, drive to practices, and still lead a regional team from behind a laptop. Life had rhythm, even if it was busy.

Then, one afternoon, the rhythm broke. His mother called, sounding strange, her speech slurred, her thoughts scattered. The neurologist later called it a "mild stroke," but the word *mild* didn't match what Mark saw in her hospital bed. Her right hand trembled as she tried to sign the discharge papers.

The family decided she shouldn't live alone anymore. Moving her into the spare bedroom felt temporary, even noble. Meals, medication reminders, and rides to therapy all seemed manageable, something they could juggle between meetings and carpools. His wife agreed, though not without a quiet sigh that said she already knew it wouldn't be temporary.

Care expanded month by month. The tremor worsened. Short walks turned into unsteady transfers. The stroke had taken more than mobility; it had eroded independence. Modifications to the bathroom drained the savings they'd meant for a family vacation. Mark started missing morning standups and signing off early. When the next round of promotions came out, his name wasn't on the list. The call from his boss was polite but direct: "You've got to be fully available to lead."

At home, the strain deepened. His wife managed meals and medications when he couldn't, but the tension sat between them like a silent guest. Their teens kept their grades up and rarely complained, yet Mark noticed the changes: the canceled tournaments, the laughter that had gone missing at dinner. Even lighthearted jokes about Grandma staying "forever" carried an edge of fatigue.

He didn't resent the care. He loved his mother deeply, but love had become complicated, a constant negotiation between duty and desire, between the people who raised him and the family he was raising. Each role demanded more than he could give. Son. Husband. Father.

Employee. There was no version of the day when someone didn't need more of him.

The house stayed full, the calendar stayed crowded, and the weight of responsibility became something he carried without noticing. That is, until moments like this, lying awake in the quiet hours, wondering how long he could hold everything together.

The Hidden Problems

Mark's situation surfaced challenges that many families face when a parent moves in for care:

1. Career impact from reduced availability and missed promotion cycles.
2. Unplanned spending from personal savings to cover gaps in care, equipment, and transportation.
3. Absence of a written care plan that shares duties across family, paid help, and community resources.
4. Safety and home-modification needs that escalate over time.
5. Care "scope creep," where responsibilities grow from reminders to full activities of daily living without a reset.
6. Strain on the marriage and on the teenagers' schedules, privacy, and opportunities.
7. Limited respite and recovery time for the primary caregiver.
8. Unclear or outdated legal tools for medical decisions and finances.
9. Confusion about benefits, including what Medicare covers, what it does not, and when to evaluate Medicaid or long-term care options.

10. Record-keeping, receipts, and documentation that lag behind real life, creating tax and reimbursement headaches.

None of these is unusual. Many are predictable. Planning early helps convert improvisation into intention.

After the Wake-Up

Mark wanted to keep his career viable, protect his marriage, support his kids, and give his mother the dignity she deserved. He created a weekly care schedule that included his spouse and a part-time aide. He met with an elder law attorney to update powers of attorney and discuss future options. He reworked the family budget and set a threshold for when to bring in additional paid support. He blocked one evening a week for the kids, no cancellations. He built a brief "handoff" checklist so his spouse or a helper could step in without chaos.

Why People Like Mark Make These Sacrifices

Love for a parent is powerful. A sense of duty can be equally strong. Families step in because it feels right and because the alternatives feel unacceptable. Motivation rarely needs to be questioned. The role itself deserves respect.

The goal is simple and firm: make clear, informed decisions that align care with values, protect the household, and keep the caregiver from disappearing inside the job. Care is an act of love. It also requires a plan that is sustainable.

Just Take Our Time

Nick and Jamie were in their early 60s when they walked into my office. Nick had worked nearly 40 years in a factory and was ready to claim his pension. With Social Security, their bills were covered. Now they wanted to turn their $300,000 in savings into "fun money."

When I asked what they envisioned for retirement, they smiled.

"We love RV trips, especially the National Parks. We've always traveled, even when the kids were little. Nick's motorcycle gets us all over Michigan. Now we want to take our time, see the whole country."

Here's the key takeaway:
Nick and Jamie didn't wait until retirement to start enjoying life. Travel and time together were already embedded in their lifestyle.

They didn't have millions saved. But thanks to a pension and years of prioritizing experiences over "someday," their plan worked.

Not everyone has a pension anymore, but everyone can decide to live with intention now. Waiting until later is risky, because "later" can be taken away.

Ask yourself:
Did Nick and Jamie watch their parents grow older and miss out?
Did they see retirement cut short by illness or, worse, regret?

Maybe that's why they prioritized time, travel, and connection over maximizing account balances.
Maybe they understood: **Time is wealth, too.**

Their story sets up our exploration of retirement lifestyle, income distribution, and how to make sure your "go-go years" don't turn into "no-go years" too soon.

Common Misconceptions

Myth: "I don't need to look at long-term care. My health is fine."
Fact: That's *exactly* when to look. Long-term care coverage is based on age and health. Waiting until you "need it" often makes it unaffordable or unavailable. Starting early means your policy can grow and keep up with inflation.

Myth: "I'm reducing investment risk to protect my money in retirement." **Fact:** This worked when retirees had guaranteed pensions and didn't rely on investments for income. Today, your portfolio may need to *generate* income for decades. The key is matching your investments to your withdrawal strategy, not just playing defense.
Myth: "I have to pay for my kids' college." **Fact:** Tuition is one of the most common retirement killers. You must ask: *Can we afford both?* That's a family conversation worth having.

Rethink Risk: Understanding Risk in Retirement Planning

"Risk" is one of the most overused and misunderstood words in retirement planning. Too often it gets treated as a single concept, when, in reality, there are two very different kinds of risk you need to consider: **risk tolerance** and **risk capacity.**

Risk Tolerance: How We Feel

Risk tolerance is emotional. It's how you react to uncertainty in the markets, news headlines, or sudden swings in your portfolio. It's your gut response to the question, *"How much risk can I live with?"*

- Based on your **age, experience, and goals**
- Driven by your **comfort level** with market fluctuations
- Varies from person to person, and can change over time
- Determines whether you panic during downturns or stay steady

Risk tolerance is personal. It's about emotions, not numbers.

Risk Capacity: What We Can Afford

Risk capacity is material and measurable. It's the objective side of the equation, focused on what your financial situation actually allows. Capacity answers the question, *How much risk can I technically afford to take?*

- Driven by **asset levels, debts, and liquidity**
- Calculated based on your **time horizon and goals**
- Evaluates the **range of outcomes** and portfolio allocation needed
- Ignores feelings; it's strictly about facts and math

Why Both Matter

The challenge and the art of retirement planning is balancing the two. If your tolerance is low but your capacity is high, you may miss opportunities by playing it too safe. If your tolerance is high but your capacity is low, you risk overexposing yourself to losses you can't recover from.

A clear plan doesn't just ask *how you feel* about risk. It also measures *how much risk you can afford to take* and then finds the right balance between the two.

With your tolerance and capacity clear, we can now design the allocation and drawdown plan that fits both your nerves and your numbers.

This is Our Legacy

"Popcorn! Get your popcorn!"
The echo of the vendor's voice mixes with the buzz of the crowd as Rod and Cindy wave from the bleachers. Their youngest son glides across the ice in his college jersey, the same number he wore in high school. Cindy claps, Rod shouts encouragement, and for a moment,

the years of practices, hotel weekends, and early mornings feel entirely worth it.

It hadn't always felt this clear.

Just a few years earlier, Rod and Cindy were sitting in my office with a different question on their minds. They were in their mid-fifties, with two sons in high school, both standout travel athletes dreaming of scholarships. Rod was an executive earning $200,000 a year, and Cindy worked part-time at a local school. Life was full, stable, and busy.

When Rod received a $200,000 bonus, he asked a simple, but weighty question: *Should we use this for college or invest it toward retirement?*

The math pointed one way. If they invested the money, an early retirement looked achievable. If they paid for college, they'd likely need to work several more years.

The numbers only tell part of the story. When we talked about their values, the answer came into focus. Their happiest memories were on the road together: tournament weekends, team dinners, the shared thrill of watching their boys grow. Supporting college wasn't just an expense; it was an extension of what made their family close.

They decided to fund college and delay retirement, investing conservatively, rather than focusing on growth for retirement. After the investments were set up, Rod was still a bit in shock. *No advisor has ever told us it was okay to choose memories over math.*

Now, years later, as he and Cindy cheer from the stands, that decision looks less like a delay and more like a dividend, the return on investing in what mattered most.

Here's the truth: Good planning doesn't follow formulas. It follows your values, but it still requires clarity about the trade-offs.

So, when at a crossroads like this, you must weigh the options and alternatives:

- Will you resent delaying retirement?
- Will you pressure your child to succeed academically or athletically?
- Will you worry if tuition rises or your child changes majors?
- What if they aren't ready or don't graduate on time?

Funding education is a deeply personal decision, but it has *real* consequences. Make sure it aligns with your long-term goals, not just short-term emotions.

It's All for Her

Jack and Diane (yes, really) came to see me with their daughter Anna, age 35, who is developmentally disabled and functions like a 10-year-old. Anna brought crayons and quietly colored during our meeting. At the end, she gave me a picture of flowers. This was the nicest gift I'd ever received, and I placed it on my office wall.

Before their next visit, I asked if Anna had a favorite snack. "Cookies," they said. So next time, I laid out a full cookie buffet. She lit up.

Cute story. But for Jack and Diane, retirement planning was anything but a lighthearted endeavor. At 70 and 55, their biggest concern wasn't traveling or downsizing. It was making sure Anna would be okay if something happened to them.

We set up income strategies, retirement plans, and most importantly, a Special Needs Trust to protect Anna's future.

If you're a parent, you understand how strong that love is. But if you're a **caretaker**, or **might be one someday**, this story foreshadows the depth of planning required, not just financially, but emotionally. It connects to the caregiving and long-term care conversations.

You're not alone, and there *is* a way to plan for everyone you love.

Clarity Affirmations

- Now I know retirement is a transition, not just a date.
- I can balance both risks and opportunities with preparation.
- I understand that money and meaning both matter.
- I will talk openly with my spouse about our expectations.

Action Plan

1. **Review** long-term care coverage options (self-fund, insure, or Medicaid).
2. **Evaluate** your investment strategy for income and growth.
3. **Talk** as a family about college vs. retirement trade-offs.
4. **Catch-up** on retirement contributions if you're over 50.
5. **Start** charitable giving conversations.
6. **Begin** or finalize formal estate planning.

Looking Ahead

Retirement prep isn't just about numbers.
It's about **choices, values, and intentions.**
The best plans are rooted in the life you want, not the life you're told to chase.

As we move into Chapter 4, we'll explore how to turn those plans into reality, making sure your "go-go years" stay that way as long as possible, and that your financial, emotional, and relational wealth are all working in harmony.

CHAPTER FOUR

Retirement Overview: Life After Work

"Do not go gentle into that good night, but rage, rage against the dying of the light."

Dylan Thomas

Retirement isn't just the end of your working years. It's the beginning of a season that can stretch for 20, 30, or even 40 years. It's a season that's shaped as much by your choices as by your circumstances.

By now, we've walked through the habits built in your 20s to 40s and the preparations made in your 50s and early 60s, so this is where it all comes together. The health of your accounts, your body, your relationships, and your sense of purpose now will determine how the next chapter unfolds.

The truth? Most people don't retire once. They enter retirement, adjust, reimagine, and adapt again, sometimes more than once. This is not a static chapter of life; it's a series of transitions. Life events, health changes, and economic shifts can all push you to reimagine your plans.

The Reality of Aging

Whether retirement starts at 55, 65, or later, the years ahead will be influenced by both the things you can control and those you can't. Here's the hard facts most don't want to hear:

- Over 38% of adult men and women over age 60 are obese (CDC).

- Over 71% of adults over 65 deal with hypertension (CDC), causing 1 in 3 deaths.
- Over 7 million Americans live with Alzheimer's, according to the Alzheimer's Association.
- The average age of death in the U.S. is 84 (CDC).
- According to the NIH, 42% of Americans over age 55 will develop dementia.
- More than 2 million Americans are over age 90, and that number is set to quadruple by 2060 (US Census Bureau).
- Research from Harvard University says there can be over 17 million households over age 80 by 2038, nearly double the current number.
- Around 90,000 people in the U.S. are centenarians and live to 100 or beyond (Boston University Medical Campus).

How well we age is shaped by many factors: sleep, smoking, diet, stress, alcohol use, sun exposure, and pollution. You *can* control some of these. Others, like your family history and genetic makeup, are out of your hands. But understanding these risks early helps you prepare for what's ahead.

Sell It and Give It Away

Let me introduce you to Don. He came into our office to review his accounts. When I asked my usual question, "What brings you in today?" Don gave me an answer I'll never forget.

> *"I'm 70 now. I met with another advisor four years ago. He said I had enough to retire… but I didn't feel ready, so I kept working. Finally retired last year to max out Social Security. My wife and I sat on the porch with a glass of Merlot to celebrate. We were talking about all the things we wanted to do. Then the cancer came. Six months later, she was gone. Now I'm selling everything and giving the money away. I just can't stay in that house."*

Don had over $2 million in savings. Social Security covered all of his living expenses, but what he wanted most, time with his wife, was gone.

His story is not about numbers; it's about how easily plans can overlook the fragile, unpredictable nature of life. Retirement isn't just about waiting until you're "ready." It's about balancing tomorrow's security with today's opportunities.

Don's story is heartbreaking, but his story isn't rare. Throughout this book, we've discussed how the quantitative (numbers) and qualitative (values) must align. Don's plan worked on paper, but emotionally and spiritually, it was incomplete.

Many retirees delay living fully, hoping to reach some magic financial milestone, but life doesn't always cooperate.

Don's advisor may have missed three essential conversations:

1. **How do you *feel* about money and work?**
2. **What does retirement success mean to *you*?**
3. **What does quality of life look like now, not just later?**

Life Happens Beyond the Numbers

Money creates options. It can protect you from hardship, but it's not the whole story.

In the last chapter, we met Nick and Jamie, who didn't wait to "start" retirement when they stopped working. Travel and connection were already part of their lives, and that made the transition smoother.

Don's story and theirs highlight the same truth: your plan should work in real life, not just in a spreadsheet.

You can't control disease or death, but you can define what "enough" looks like and be available for what matters, *now*.

A fully wealthy life includes:

- Financial independence
- A purpose beyond work
- Strong relationships
- A legacy of intention

The Three Phases of Retirement

Just as seasons change, our retirement does as well. These phases aren't always neatly divided, but they do follow a general pattern.

1. **Go-Go Years**
   You're active, independent, and full of energy. You may travel, volunteer, babysit grandkids, serve on boards, or work part-time. For many, these are the best years of retirement.

2. **Slow-Go Years**
   Energy starts to decline. You may do fewer activities or need some help. Medical needs increase. You stay closer to home but still maintain independence.

3. **No-Go Years**
   Mobility, cognition, or health challenges reduce your independence. This stage often requires home care, assisted living, or nursing care. Planning ahead is crucial (see Chapters 5 and 9).

Your story might not follow this script exactly. But planning for each phase allows you to live with dignity and purpose through all of them.

Retirement planning must prepare for each stage, with compassion, flexibility, and a willingness to pivot.

Longevity and Health: The Two Big Unknowns

- **Longevity Risk**: You don't know how long you'll live. Planning only to 75 can leave you short at 85 or 95.
- **Health Risk**: You don't know how well you'll live. Good health habits and early decisions about care can ease future burdens. This is why we emphasize habits early and why we devote entire chapters to Medicare, Medicaid, and caregiving.

Neither can be predicted with certainty, but both can be prepared for with intention and flexibility.

We use age 90 as a baseline in most plans unless there's a medical reason not to. With more people living into their 90s and beyond, it's critical to make your money and health last.

Both are unpredictable, which is why your plan needs to bend without breaking.

Retirement doesn't change who you are; it magnifies it.

It comes down to habits, mindset, and relationships. How did you care for your health?

- Did you build community or isolate?
- Did you develop purpose beyond work?
- Did you prepare financially, or wing it?

The seeds that were sown in the accumulation and prep phases bear fruit here. Retirement reveals your true wealth, or lack of it.

When to Take Social Security

This is one of the most impactful decisions you'll make.

Myth: "I'll take Social Security as soon as I'm eligible. Who knows how long I'll live?"
Fact: Taking it early could mean:

- Going *back* to work
- Drawing more heavily from your savings
- Risking a lower quality of life later

Myth: "I'll wait until age 70 to get the max benefit."
Fact: That's only necessary *if* you truly need the additional income *and* don't have other reliable sources (like pensions or investments).

The best timing depends on:

- Your health
- Your life expectancy
- Your other income sources
- Your goals

Other Sources of Predictable Income

- Pensions
- Deferred compensation
- Annuities
- Dividend-paying investments
- Retiree benefits

Pensions, deferred compensation, annuities, dividend income, and retiree benefits all create stability. The more predictable your income, the less stress you'll feel when markets fluctuate.

We'll revisit distribution strategies and tax considerations in later chapters, but here's the key: income should be structured so you can maintain your lifestyle without living in constant fear of market swings.

What About Roth Conversions?

Myth: "I should convert all my IRA/401(k) into a Roth."
Fact: That creates an immediate tax bill, sometimes massive. It *can* make sense if:

- You plan to leave a tax-free legacy
- You're retiring early (60s) and expect to live long (90+)
- You'll benefit from tax-free growth over decades

Here's what we *don't* do: Convert a large amount and then invest it all in bonds or cash. (Yes, I've seen it.) That slows down your ability to recoup the taxes you just paid.

Smart conversions are phased, intentional, and tied to your legacy planning.

Retirement Investing: The Bucket Strategy

Your portfolio generates growth in retirement. In order to turn that growth into spendable income, you need to sell some of your holdings. The mantra "Buy low. Sell high" is our go-to. The problem occurs when you have to sell low. You need money to pay bills, no matter what happens in the market. This causes a lot of fear when people are losing money in the portfolio AND drawing it down at the same time. It's hard to sail a ship that's sinking from a leak you can't plug. To keep your ship afloat, even during storms, I use the **bucket strategy**.

Bucket 1: Cash
Enough to cover 12 to 24 months of expenses.

Bucket 2: Income
Investments that provide steady, predictable income to replenish your cash.

Bucket 3: Growth
Long-term investments are designed for appreciation.

This strategy creates a spending and income cushion, so you don't have to sell stocks at a loss during market downturns. Instead, you draw from cash and income, giving your growth investments time to recover.

We'll revisit this in later chapters, especially when discussing funding long-term care and leaving a legacy.

Charitable Giving, Legacy, and Purpose

In Chapter 8, we'll explore charitable giving in detail. But the heart of that conversation starts here.

Ask yourself:

- **What do I want my legacy to be?**
- **Do I want to give now or later?**
- **Do I want to leave money to children, the church, or a cause I care about?**

Retirement is not just about what you take with you. It's about what you leave behind.

Clarity Affirmations

- Now I know the seasons of retirement: go-go, slow-go, and no-go.
- I can see how my time, health, and money connect.
- I understand that retirement is about purpose as well as planning.
- I will map my years with clarity and intention.

Action Plan

1. **Determine** how much income your portfolio needs to generate.
2. **Develop** a tax-smart investment, distribution, and estate strategy.
3. **Run** scenarios to determine when to take Social Security.
4. **Estimate** long-term care costs and look at coverage options.
5. **Review** longevity with various aging scenarios.
6. **Craft** a giving plan.

This plan isn't just financial. These topics create your legacy and affect your family, your future, and your peace of mind.

Retirement isn't just the finish line of your career; it's the start of your most intentional season. A time to live, to love, to give, and to reflect. This isn't the end. It's time to turn purpose into legacy.

Looking Ahead

Retirement is not the end of the road; it's a new stretch of it. The years ahead can be your most intentional, most meaningful, and most rewarding… if you enter them ready for what they may hold. The steps you take now don't just safeguard your finances; they shape your experiences, your relationships, and the legacy you leave behind.

We'll address one of the most overlooked (and expensive) parts of retirement: **taxes** and **healthcare.** Later chapters will return to many of the themes from this one: income planning, long-term care, family dynamics, and giving, through real stories of people who faced these decisions unprepared.

The best time to prepare was yesterday. The next best time is now.

Part 2: The Financial Realities of Retirement

CHAPTER FIVE
The Hidden Retirement Bill: Taxes and Withdrawals

"It's not how much you make, it's how much you keep."

Anonymous

When people picture retirement planning, they usually ask:

1. How much can I safely spend?
2. Will I run out of money?

However, there's a third question that's often overlooked that decides whether you experience clarity or crisis:
How much will I owe in taxes?

You can build a seven-figure nest egg, but if the sequence of withdrawals and tax rules aren't managed, that "million-dollar retirement" can spend like much less. In the next few chapters, we'll dive into healthcare, estate planning, caregiving, and family dynamics. Taxes sit at the center of all of them, which is why we're addressing this now, immediately after retirement. That difference can ripple across every chapter ahead—your healthcare costs, your giving, your estate plan, and even the legacy your heirs receive.

This chapter pulls those threads together. It isn't about tax trivia. It's about clarity: how to keep more of what you've earned, and avoid crises triggered by avoidable tax surprises.

Drawdown Strategy: You Control the Flow

Earlier, we used the **Bucket Strategy** to think about market risk and time horizons.

Here, I want you to picture something different: a **Cascade.** Each account type: taxable, tax-deferred, and tax-free, is like a level in that cascade. If you open the wrong level at the wrong time, the flow becomes turbulent: higher taxes, bigger Medicare premiums, more taxable Social Security. If you follow the right sequence, the water runs smoothly, predictably, and efficiently all the way down.

That's the heart of drawdown planning: deciding which cascade to release first, and which to hold until later. Done with clarity, your resources last. Done carelessly, the turbulence erodes them too quickly.

The Three Cascades of Retirement Income

Every dollar you've saved flows into one of three cascades:

1. **Tax-Deferred (Traditional)** — 401(k), Traditional IRA, 403(b), SEP IRA
    - You didn't pay taxes when you contributed.
    - Withdrawals are taxed as ordinary income.
    - Subject to Required Minimum Distributions (RMDs).
2. **Tax-Free** — Roth IRA, Roth 401(k), HSA (for health expenses)
    - You paid taxes up front.
    - Growth and qualified withdrawals are tax-free.
    - No RMDs (for Roth IRAs).
3. **Taxable** — Brokerage accounts, savings, CDs, real estate

- Subject to capital gains, dividends, and interest taxes.
- Basis (what you originally invested) matters.
- Step-up in basis at death.

Understanding which cascade to release first: taxable, tax-deferred, or tax-free, can save you tens of thousands over a lifetime.

A Simple Picture: Your Retirement Pantry

If the cascade imagery feels abstract, think of your retirement accounts like a **pantry**:

- **Taxable accounts** are like fresh produce: use them first before they spoil.
- **Tax-deferred accounts** are like frozen food: they last a long time, but eventually you have to cook them, and when you do, you share a portion with the IRS.
- **Roth accounts** are like canned goods: they stay good the longest, and when you finally open them, you keep all of it.

Here's the danger: some people say, *"I'm good; I've got Roths,"* and they eat all their canned goods first. The problem starts when the freezer food comes due, and they're forced to use it in bulk, and that's when taxes and penalties pile up.

Clarity means using each type in the right order so nothing goes to waste. Crisis comes when you consume the wrong shelf too early.

The Problem with Tax Deferral

For years, the assumption was: *"You'll be in a lower tax bracket in retirement."* As we'll see later, fewer deductions, Medicare surcharges, and taxable Social Security often push retirees into higher brackets. Surviving spouses can be hit especially hard when their income is taxed at single rates.

Deferral isn't free. Eventually, the IRS comes knocking. The real question is how to spread that tax bill across your lifetime so it doesn't show up all at once.

The Roth Conversion Myth Revisited

Earlier in the book, we confronted the myth that Roth conversions are always the right answer. They're not.

A conversion can reduce future RMDs, create tax-free income, and help heirs, but the timing must be strategic.

A poorly timed conversion can raise your Medicare premiums, increase taxable Social Security, or push you into a bracket you didn't expect, topics we'll explore in upcoming chapters.

The lesson: Roth conversions are a tool, not a silver bullet. Used with foresight, they create clarity. Used in a vacuum, they create crisis.

Ted's Story: When the Cascade Was Opened Too Soon

Ted retired at 62 with good intentions and bad guidance. His goal was to keep his tax bracket low in his "go-go" years.

So he began draining his **Roth accounts first**, thinking he was being prudent. The withdrawals were tax-free, and his advisor even praised him for "keeping taxable income down."

But there was a hidden problem. By the time Ted turned 73 and **Required Minimum Distributions (RMDs)** kicked in, his Roths were nearly empty, leaving almost everything in his **tax-deferred cascade.** Suddenly, he was slammed with taxes:

- His RMDs shoved him into a higher bracket.
- His Social Security became taxable.
- His Medicare premiums spiked two years later.

To make matters worse, years earlier, Ted had done a **large Roth conversion during his peak earning years.** That single move created tens of thousands in extra taxes, and it took him years just to recover from the hit.

Ted thought he was buying clarity by avoiding taxes early. In reality, he had simply postponed the turbulence, and when the floodgates opened, it all came crashing down at once.

The Danger of Planning in a Vacuum

This is one of the most common mistakes I see.

- A financial advisor recommends a Roth conversion.
- The client acts, thinking it's the smart move.
- Months later, their CPA is left cleaning up the mess: *"Did you realize this pushed you into a higher bracket and increased your Medicare premiums?"*

The problem isn't the concept; it's the lack of coordination.

Any taxable event: conversion, business sale, or real estate gain, should be reviewed with your tax preparer first.

Some advisors take their tax knowledge further by becoming **Enrolled Agents** (**EA**s), authorized to represent clients before the IRS. Even if your advisor isn't an EA, they should at least know how to review your **Form 1040** and use it as a roadmap, not guesswork.

The Cost Objection: "A CPA Is Too Expensive"

Some people hesitate to involve their CPA regularly because of cost, but here's the truth: the **cost of not involving them is often far greater.**

A poorly timed Roth conversion, a mismanaged capital gain, or an overlooked RMD penalty can cost **tens of thousands of dollars in**

extra taxes and Medicare premiums, far more than the price of an annual planning conversation.

Think of a CPA not as an expense, but as insurance against costly mistakes. In most cases, one well-timed piece of tax coordination pays for its fee many times over.

Questions to Ask Your Financial Advisor

- Do you review my 1040 every year?
- Do you use tax planning software to model future scenarios?
- Will you coordinate with my CPA before making recommendations?

If the answer is *no*, you may be receiving advice that sounds good in theory but creates tax headaches in practice.

This isn't a one-time choice. As we saw with Ted, circumstances change: markets, health, even tax law. That's why you revisit your drawdown annually, ideally with your advisor and CPA in the same room (or at least on the same call).

For Caregivers and POAs: The Guardian of the Cascades

If you're reading this for a spouse, parent, or loved one, you might be worried: *"This is too much. I can't be a tax expert."* Take heart. You don't have to be.

Think of it like a story.

In the kingdom of Eldara, a great river fed three magical cascades:

- The first flowed with **fresh fruits and herbs**.
- The second held **ice-bound stores** that the Guild taxed whenever they were opened.
- The last flowed from **enchanted jars**, untouched by time.

The Queen grew old, and her daughter Lyra was entrusted as **Guardian of the Cascades.** Lyra didn't know every law of the Guild or spell of taxation. She only knew this: *if she chose the wrong cascade too soon, the river would turn against the kingdom.*

One day, a villager urged her: *"Open the frozen stores now! It's easiest!"* But Lyra remembered her mother's counsel: never open a cascade alone. So, she called together the court wizard and royal steward. Together, they mapped the flow, showing that opening the frozen stores too early would trigger storms across the land: higher levies, spoiled crops, wasted reserves.

Instead, they guided the river carefully. The kingdom thrived.

Lyra sighed with relief. She didn't need to master every spell or tax code. She only needed to guard the gates and summon her team.

Translation to Real Life

Your cascades aren't magical, but financial: taxable, tax-deferred, and tax-free accounts. Like Lyra, you don't need to know every rule. You just need to guard the flow, ask the right questions, and call your team.

That's the relief: **this isn't one more thing you have to carry alone.** You can have a team: advisor, CPA, attorney, working on your behalf.

Clarity Affirmations

- Now I know how taxes affect every dollar I keep.
- I can ask my advisor the right questions about drawdown strategies.
- I understand that timing matters as much as totals.
- I will make confident decisions about my accounts.

Action Plan

1. **Identify your cascades**. Know what's taxable, tax-deferred, and tax-free.
2. **Run a tax projection**. Don't guess; model your future brackets.
3. **Revisit the Roth conversion myth**. Don't assume it's always best; weigh timing.
4. **Coordinate**. Require collaboration between your advisor, CPA, and estate attorney.
5. **Adjust annually**. Markets, tax laws, and health all change, so should your drawdown.

Looking Ahead

Now that you've done the work to plan the technical, it's time to protect it. We'll look at your care and estate plan, which are often ignored. First, let's talk to people facing some steep challenges and opportunities, entrepreneurs, and business owners.

CHAPTER SIX
Aging, Exit, and Legacy for Business Owners

"By working faithfully eight hours a day, you may eventually get to be the boss and work twelve hours a day."

Robert Frost

In the previous chapters, we explored retirement and the hidden retirement bill of taxes and withdrawals. Ahead, we'll look at estate planning, caregiving, and legacy, but for business owners, those conversations look different. The stakes are higher. The layers are more complex.

You Raised the Stakes

Founders are cut from a different cloth. You built something out of nothing: working the land, closing the deals, pulling the late nights, and signing the notes when no one else would. Independence and grit got you here, and pride keeps you pushing forward.

What you've built is more than an enterprise. It's your life's work, shaped by vision, sweat, and sacrifice. You took risks others wouldn't, created jobs, supported your family, and left your mark on a community.

But here's the paradox: the same grit that made you successful is what makes you vulnerable. The attitude of *"I'll handle it myself"* can undo everything when it comes time to transition.

Different Business Owner Mindsets

1. **The Hyper-Analytical Owner**
   All about valuations, the bottom line, and enterprise value. They'll scrutinize tax strategy, exit multiples, and legal structures, but may neglect life after business.
   Strength: Precision, structure, and financial discipline.
   Challenge: Numbers can tell you what your business is worth, but they can't tell you who you'll be when it's gone.
2. **The Heart and Soul Owner**
   Community-based, passionate, relational. The business is identity and family. Often resists delegating, documenting, or formalizing.
   Strength: Deep relationships and loyalty.
   Challenge: Passion built your business, but passion alone won't preserve it. Without systems, your life's work can vanish overnight.
3. **The Farmer**
   Independent, proud, and often values tradition over transition. Farming is lifestyle as much as business, where land is passed down, but not always structured well.
   Strength: Work ethic, perseverance, and generational pride.
   Challenge: The old ways may have built your farm, but the new realities (laws, taxes, probate, creditor risk) will decide whether it survives another generation.
4. **The Stubborn Independent**
   Believes in self-reliance: "I'll handle it myself." Avoids advisors, resists outside help, delays planning until it's too late.
   Strength: Determination and grit.
   Challenge: Independence may have built your business, but

collaboration will save it. A plan built alone rarely survives long after you're gone.

5. **The Artistic Creative**
   Brilliant, visionary, one-of-a-kind. The business reflects your artistry, creativity, or genius.
   Strength: Originality and brand identity.
   Challenge: Almost impossible to replicate or transfer unless you've trained others, documented processes, or protected intellectual property.

When There's No Plan

Every day, owners lose their life's work, not because the business failed, but because there was no plan.

- The family farm gets auctioned off when siblings can't agree.
- The real estate portfolio gets locked in probate because deeds weren't titled properly.
- The company you poured decades into is sold for pennies because your spouse or kids don't know how to run it.
- Employees who depended on you show up Monday morning to find the doors closed.

That's not legacy. That's loss. And it's avoidable.

Just like in family caregiving, something we'll explore later, failing to plan leaves loved ones to pick up the pieces, often in the middle of grief, confusion, or conflict.

Consider Jim: he ran a multimillion-dollar laundry business with his wife and father. But when his father died, the business structure hadn't been updated. When Jim died suddenly in his 50s, his widow inherited not a thriving enterprise, but chaos: grieving employees, vendor contracts, and mounting debt. Without a roadmap, the business, and much of the legacy, collapsed.

Jim's story didn't have to end this way. Neither does yours.

What Do We Mean by Exit and Succession Planning?

Think of the process in layers:

Exit Planning → big picture: financial + personal goals
↓
Succession Planning → who leads, trains, transitions
↓
Valuation → know your worth, track growth, tax prep
↓
Transition → sale, transfer, phased retirement
↓
Risk Management → protection against "what ifs"

5-4-3-2-1 Exit Planning: Lessons for Business Owners

According to the Exit Planning Institute (EPI), roughly 80% of many owners' net worth is tied up in their business. For most, the company isn't just an income source, it's their largest asset and the key to funding life after exit. That's why exit planning isn't just about selling the business; it's about creating what Christopher Snider calls a *"significant company"* in his book *Walking to Destiny.*

The Five Stages of Value Maturity

Snider outlines a framework called the **Value Maturity Index**, a process that moves an owner from simply running a business to creating transferable value:

1. **Identify** – Determine your baseline business value. A formal valuation helps highlight both strengths and vulnerabilities.

2. **Protect** – Safeguard that value against risks like the "5 D's": death, disability, divorce, distress, and disagreement.
3. **Build** – Increase value by strengthening cash flow and improving both tangible and intangible assets (human, social, customer, and structural capital).
4. **Harvest** – Decide how and when to transition. This could be a sale, a family succession, or simply reaping the rewards of greater profitability.
5. **Manage** – Align both personal and financial goals during and after the exit, ensuring sustainability for your next act.

The Four Intangible Capitals

EPI emphasizes that 80% of a company's value often lies in what can't be easily measured on a balance sheet — the **4 Cs**:

- **Human Capital**: Your people and leadership talent.
- **Social Capital**: Culture, values, and how your team works together.
- **Customer Capital**: Depth and durability of customer relationships.
- **Structural Capital**: Processes, systems, and intellectual property that make the business run without owner dependence.

The Three Gaps and the Three Legs

Exit planning also involves addressing three critical gaps:

- **Wealth Gap**: The difference between what you have and what you need to live your desired post-exit life.

- **Profit Gap**: The gap between your business's current performance and best-in-class standards.
- **Value Gap**: The difference between what your business is worth today and what it could be worth with improvements.

These are supported by the "**Three Legs of the Stool**": balancing business planning, personal financial planning, and personal purpose. Without balance, the stool topples.

Two Paths, One Goal

Finally, EPI stresses that owners must walk **two concurrent paths**: improving the business while simultaneously preparing for life after it. Too many owners only work *in* the business, not *on* it, leaving them unprepared for a meaningful "next act." The ultimate goal of exit planning isn't just to sell; it's to build a company that is both attractive to buyers and ready for transition. That's what makes a company *significant.*

Exit Planning

Exit planning is the process of preparing for the day you step away from your business, whether by retirement, sale, disability, or death. It ensures you, your family, and your employees are financially secure when you do. A strong exit plan covers:

- How and when you'll step back
- How ownership will be sold, transferred, or passed on
- How to protect business value during the process
- How personal financial goals align with the transition

Succession Planning

Succession is about *people*, not just ownership papers. It identifies future leaders, trains them, and builds a team that can carry the business forward without disruption. Without it, even the strongest balance sheet can collapse.

Valuation

You can't plan your exit without knowing what the business is worth. A valuation is more than a number—it's a mirror. It shows the health of your business, its strengths, and its vulnerabilities. Regular valuations let you track growth, prepare taxes, and negotiate from strength.

Transition

Transition is the bridge between you running the business and someone else carrying it forward. It can take the form of:

- A sale to a third party
- A transfer to family or key employees
- A phased retirement where you gradually step back

The smoother the transition, the less disruption it causes for employees, customers, and their families.

Risk Management

No plan is complete without protection against the "what ifs." As we'll see in the estate planning chapter, your business plan and your personal plan must align. Gaps in one create vulnerabilities in the other.

Tool	**Purpose**
Key Person Insurance	Protects the business financially if you or another vital leader dies unexpectedly.
Buy-Sell Agreements	Sets clear rules between partners or heirs for ownership transfer.
Legal Structures	Minimizes tax burdens and protects business assets.
Contingency Plans	Prepares for illness, disability, or sudden death to ensure continuity.

The Value of the Owner

A business isn't just buildings and balance sheets. Much of its value is tied to *you*. Decades of trust in the community, relationships with bankers, vendors, clients, and customers, and deep industry knowledge form an invisible asset.

But here's the danger: if all that value lives only in you, it disappears the moment you step away.

That's why the shift matters: are you working *in* the business, or *on* the business? Owners buried in day-to-day tasks make themselves indispensable, but also unsellable. Owners who build systems, empower leaders, and document processes create value that lasts beyond them.

When All the Value Walks Out the Door

For forty years, Mary's Diner was a cornerstone of the community. Everyone knew Mary. Her recipes brought people in, her smile kept them coming back, and her leadership made the diner run like clockwork.

But when Mary passed unexpectedly, the truth surfaced: there was no "diner" without Mary. Her recipes weren't written down. Vendor relationships lived only in her Rolodex. Staff turnover spiked. Within a year, the doors closed.

The diner wasn't sold for pennies; it wasn't sold at all. Because everything that made it valuable left with Mary.

This is the difference between **lifestyle value** and **enterprise value**. Lifestyle value depends on *you*. Enterprise value exists when the business can thrive without you.

Ask yourself:

- Could my business run for six months without me?
- Are systems and processes documented, or only in my head?
- Do customers come for the brand, or for me?
- Is leadership spread across a team, or concentrated in one person?
- Would revenue continue tomorrow if I walked away today?

Different Kinds of Business Owners, Different Challenges

Not every business owner looks the same, and neither do their succession challenges.

- **The All-In Founder**: Identity bound to the company. Letting go feels like losing a piece of themselves.
- **The Serial Entrepreneur**: Multiple enterprises—each with different exit paths. The challenge is coordination.

- **The Hybrid Owner-Employee**: Works a W-2 job and runs a side business. Challenge: separating authority and finances.
- **The New-Age Entrepreneur**: Royalties, courses, YouTube, or social media income. Challenge: documenting and protecting intangible, algorithm-driven revenue streams.

Each type has a different vulnerability, but the principle is the same: if the business can't thrive without you, it may not be worth much when you're gone.

Common Myths About Business Exits

Business owners often fall into traps of false confidence. Here are the myths I hear most:

1. **"My business is worth 3–4x revenue."**
   The "country club valuation." In reality, valuation depends on industry, size, and structure. True value comes from what the business is worth *without you.*

2. **"I can exit within a year."**
   Maybe, but not if you want maximum value. It usually takes 3–5 years to prepare, clean up operations, and train leadership.

3. **"I'll just sell to private equity or venture capital."**
   Unless your enterprise value exceeds $50–100 million, you'll need other options, such as family succession, management buyouts, ESOPs, or installment sales.

4. **"My kids will just take it over."**
   Do they even want to? Are they equipped? Will customers and employees trust them? Legacy doesn't transfer by last name alone. If your exit plan is just 'my kids will figure it out,'

congratulations, you've created the most stressful group project of their lives.

5. **"My advisor will guide me through succession."** Most advisors excel at managing funds after the sale, not guiding the years-long process of preparation, negotiation, and transition. Don't assume they'll handle it unless you've asked hard questions.

Life After the Exit: More Than a Transaction

An exit isn't the finish line. It's the beginning of a new chapter.

Much like the retirement planning we discussed earlier, life after business ownership requires a vision beyond finances. Without purpose, even a well-funded retirement can feel empty.

For many owners, the business has been more than income; it's been identity. You thought about it after hours, took calls on weekends, and carried it with you on vacations. So, when it's gone, the space doesn't stay empty. Without preparation, it fills with regret, restlessness, or depression.

That's why true succession planning goes beyond logistics. It's about building a *new identity post-sale.*

Ask yourself:

- Who am I without the business?
- What will give me purpose?
- How will I invest my time, energy, and relationships once the calls stop coming?

Some find fulfillment in mentoring or philanthropy. Others finally pursue passions, such as travel, hobbies, or causes they've put off for decades. The point is: decide in advance.

Your exit is not the end of your story. It's the prologue to the next one.

From Awareness to Action

By now, you've identified your mindset as an owner, thought honestly about the type of business you run, dispelled some common myths, and seen how exit planning unfolds in stages. You've also considered what life after the business might look like.

That's the foundation. The next step is turning awareness into action. In the following section, we'll move into the **"how"**, the practical strategies, tools, and conversations that transform a fragile plan into a legacy that lasts.

Your Next Step: The Succession Guide (available to download at Claritybeforecrisis.com)

I created the **Business Owner Succession Guide** as a practical resource for owners like you. It walks through:

- **Succession & Exit Planning** — Buy-Sell Agreements, Key Person Insurance, Installment Sales.
- **Leadership Continuity** — how to build a real team instead of a single point of failure.
- **Financial & Legal Protection** — aligning your entity structure, estate plan, and insurance.
- **Real Estate & Rental Planning** — avoiding probate traps and management gaps.

It also covers **exit strategies, the 10 pillars of a successful exit, and a simple one-page succession plan** you can start on today.

Why It Matters

This chapter is about *why*. Why planning is important and what can happen if you don't. The guide is about *how*. Don't wait. Use it.

Clarity Affirmations

- Now I know my business is more than numbers; it's my legacy.
- I can protect both my family and my employees through planning.
- I understand that lasting value depends on systems, not just me.
- I will envision and prepare for life after ownership.

Action Plan for Business Owners

Just as every chapter ends with action steps, here's your checklist:

1. **Get a business valuation**
2. **Establish a written succession plan**
3. **Create or update a buy-sell agreement**
4. **Set up key person insurance**
5. **Coordinate legal documents with your estate plan**
6. **Discuss family involvement openly and honestly**
7. **Work with an exit planning team early**
8. **Document your processes and vendor contacts**
9. **Evaluate how real estate fits into your estate**
10. **Envision life after business ownership, and plan for it**

Final Thoughts

Planning for aging, caregiving, and estate matters, topics we'll explore later, brings clarity to families. For business owners, planning your exit brings the same clarity to your life's work.

You've poured decades into building something meaningful: jobs, relationships, a reputation in your community. Don't let that value evaporate because of delay or denial. Treat your business transition with the same care you've given your employees, your customers, and your family.

Retirement or succession isn't about letting go—it's about passing the baton. It's about transforming years of grit and sacrifice into something that lasts beyond you. It's about protecting both enterprise value *and* personal legacy.

Your exit is not the end of your story. It's the beginning of the next opportunity for you, your business, and the people who carry it forward.

Looking Ahead

A self-employed business owner received a nice exemption on their health insurance, but now that exemption is going away. You're no longer paying for office supplies and equipment, so now it's about deciding how you make sure your health is cared for.

CHAPTER SEVEN
Paying for Healthcare: Medicare Overview

"It is health that is real wealth and not pieces of gold and silver."

Mahatma Gandhi

Healthcare is one of the most critical components of a retirement plan, and often the most misunderstood. If you've been to a foreign country and didn't know the language, you probably felt completely lost. Making a mistake in health coverage will cause more pain than spicy Indian food. Now, you can travel to the exotic destination of healthcare planning because you have an interpreter.

In previous chapters, we emphasized the role of **health** in the True Wealth equation. Now we begin translating that principle into strategy. You'll see why the best-laid financial plans can collapse without proper health coverage, and how you can prevent that outcome.

This chapter focuses on **Medicare**, the government-run program that most retirees rely on. In the next chapter, we'll cover **Medicaid**, which comes into play for long-term care and financial hardship.

While these two are often confused, they serve vastly different purposes. Understanding the difference and when each applies will save you confusion, stress, and money.

Joe's Journey

At 64, Joe felt a rollercoaster of emotions. He'd saved well and was on track for a comfortable retirement, but as a diabetic, he dreaded choosing an affordable health plan.

When it came to Medicare, Joe saw two options:

1. **Get sold.**
2. **Get smart.**

He chose smart. A quick YouTube search taught him the basics of Medicare. He joined a Facebook group of people navigating the same decisions and connected with a counselor who factored in his health needs and travel plans.

By the time his enrollment period arrived, Joe was confident. He ignored the flood of scare tactics and sales calls. He had a plan and better things to do, like booking his next trip.

The Healthcare Shift in Retirement

If you've spent decades on employer-sponsored health insurance, retirement can feel like stepping into a foreign country. You're not alone. Most retirees are overwhelmed by:

- Unfamiliar language (Parts A, B, C, D)
- Confusing enrollment windows
- Rising costs
- Coverage gaps

Healthcare costs in retirement are rising 7% annually, so the stakes are high. According to recent data, the average couple retiring today will spend over **$300,000** out of pocket on healthcare in retirement. That doesn't include long-term care.

Don't worry. We'll break it down. Special thanks to **Joanne Giardini-Russell and the Giardini Medicare team** for their expert insight.

Medicare vs. Medicaid: A Preview

- **Medicare** is for those over age 65 (or disabled). It covers doctor visits, hospital stays, and prescription drugs, with options to add supplemental coverage. It is income-tested but not asset-tested.

- **Medicaid** is for people with limited income and assets. It can cover long-term care, including nursing homes, which Medicare does *not* fully cover. More on this upcoming.

You might never need Medicaid, but knowing how it works can be critical if circumstances change.

Medicare Basics

What Is Medicare?

Medicare is a federal health insurance program, administered by the **Centers for Medicare and Medicaid Services (CMS)**. Not to be confused with Medicaid (which is state-run), Medicare serves older adults and individuals with certain disabilities.

Myth: Medicare covers everything.
Fact: It doesn't. That's why supplement plans exist: to cover the "gaps" left behind.

When Are You Eligible?

- **At age 65** for most people.
- **After 24 months of receiving Social Security Disability** benefits.
- **Immediately** if you have ALS or end-stage renal disease.

The Initial Enrollment Period (IEP) begins **three months before** your 65th birthday and ends **three months after**.
If you're still working, you might delay **Part B** until retirement without penalty, but only if you meet specific criteria. Consult a Medicare agent before deferring.

Breaking Down the Parts of Medicare

Part A – Hospital Insurance

- Covers: Inpatient care, skilled nursing, hospice, and limited home health.
- Premium: Usually **free** (if you or your spouse paid Medicare taxes for 10+ years).
- Out-of-pocket: Deductibles and coinsurance based on your **benefit period**, not a yearly deductible.

Part B – Medical Insurance

- Covers: Doctor visits, outpatient care, durable medical equipment, and preventive services.
- Premium: Most people pay monthly.
- Additional costs: Annual deductible and 20% coinsurance.

Part C – Medicare Advantage

- Combines Parts A & B (often Part D too).
- Offered by **private insurers**.
- May include extra benefits (dental, vision, hearing).
- Requires use of **in-network providers**.

Part D – Prescription Drug Coverage

- Covers: Prescription drugs.
- Optional, but recommended to avoid future penalties.
- Offered via standalone plans or Medicare Advantage.

Medigap vs. Medicare Advantage

A common source of confusion: **Medigap** and **Medicare Supplement** are two terms for the *same thing*.

These are private insurance plans that fill the coverage gaps in Original Medicare (Parts A and B), such as deductibles, co-pays, and coinsurance.

- **Medigap Plans**: Standardized (Plans A–N), offer nationwide coverage, and allow you to see any doctor who accepts Medicare
- **Medicare Advantage (Part C)**: May be cheaper, but restricts you to provider networks and often requires pre-approvals

Choosing between these options depends on your health needs, location, travel plans, and budget. Weigh them carefully and seek guidance if needed.

How Much Will Medicare Cost?

IRMAA: Income-Related Monthly Adjustment Amount

Your Part B and D premiums are adjusted based on your **income two years prior**. For example, your 2025 premiums are based on your 2023 Modified Adjusted Gross Income (MAGI).

Single	Married filing jointly	Part B IRMAA	Part D IRMAA
Less than or equal to $106,000	Less than or equal to $212,000	$0.00	$0.00
$106,000-$133,000	$212,000-$266,000	$74.00	$13.70
$133,000-$167,000	$266,000-$334,000	$185.00	$35.30

$167,000-$200,000	$334,000-$400,000	$295.90	$57.00
$200,000-$500,000	$400,000-$750,000	$406.90	$78.60
$500,000 +	$750,000+	$443.90	$85.80

See the above IRMAA income brackets for 2025. This is why tax planning in retirement is crucial. Roth conversions, capital gains, and even RMDs (Required Minimum Distributions) can push you into a higher bracket.

Medicare is great, until you need more than what it offers

Here's where many people get caught off guard. Medicare **does not cover**:

- Long-term care (nursing homes, assisted living)
- Dental, vision, and hearing (except for certain exceptions)
- Custodial care (help with bathing, dressing, eating), except after hospitalization
- Most prescription glasses, dentures, or hearing aids

We've explored some strategies to address these gaps, but for now, know this:

Short-Term Care: Filling the Gap Medicare Leaves

Something happens. You fall, have surgery, or face an illness that leaves you needing help at home. You might not need years of extended care, but you do need support right now. That could mean a home health aide to help with bathing and meals, a short stay in rehab, or extra assistance so your family can keep working while you recover.

This is exactly where Medicare falls short. Medicare may cover some skilled care after a hospital stay, but it does not cover the day-to-day, non-medical assistance that most people actually need.

Short-Term Care Insurance is designed to fill that gap. Think of it like the AFLAC commercials: it pays for the things your health insurance or Medicare does not. Policies typically cover up to 12 months of care and can help pay for:

- In-home aides after surgery or illness
- Assisted living or rehab stays during recovery
- Respite care for family caregivers

For many families, short-term care becomes the bridge between Medicare's limited coverage and the reality of needing help. It can also be a lifeline for those who cannot qualify for long-term care insurance or who want a more affordable way to protect themselves against immediate risks.

Planning Point: Short-term care will not replace a long-term care strategy, but it can prevent a health setback from becoming a budgetary crisis. It answers the question, *"How do we pay for the help we suddenly need?"*

Hospitalization & Medicare

If you're hospitalized under Medicare Part A:

- You pay a **deductible** first.
- Then **coinsurance** is based on the length of stay.
- Medicare covers up to **60 Lifetime Reserve Days** (after your standard benefit is exhausted).
- Benefit periods are **not calendar-based**; they reset after a 60-day break in care.

Medicare Advantage plans may have different rules for hospital coverage. Be sure to understand your specific plan.

Important: Original Medicare **does not cover** dental, vision, hearing aids, or prescriptions. Consider supplemental policies for these needs.

Annual Notice of Change (ANOC)

Each fall, your Medicare Advantage or Part D plan will send you an **Annual Notice of Change** (ANOC). This outlines changes to **premiums, coverage, and provider networks** for the upcoming year. Review this carefully!

Myth: Medicare Covers Long-Term Care **Fact:** Medicare only covers **short-term skilled nursing** following hospitalization.

For **long-term care**, Medicaid may help, but only after you've **spent down** your assets. (We'll cover this as we discuss long-term care planning and Medicaid.) See the table at the end of this chapter.

Dual Eligibility: Medicare + Medicaid

Some individuals qualify for both Medicare and Medicaid. These are called **"Dual Eligibles"** and may qualify for special **D-SNP** (Dual Special Needs Plans), which coordinate benefits across both programs.

Income matters for both Medicare costs and Medicaid eligibility.

Special Situations to Watch For

You may need tailored Medicare advice if:

- You have retiree coverage through your employer.
- You're working for a small business that is not required to provide insurance.

- You're leaving an **Affordable Care Act** plan.
- You're currently using **COBRA** coverage.

In these cases, coordinated planning is essential. This is important for other topics, such as Medicaid and Senior Care.

Clarity Affirmations

- Now I know healthcare costs are a key part of retirement.
- I can see how Medicare fits into my plan.
- I understand the difference between preparation and crisis.
- I will protect both my health and my wealth.

Action Plan

1. **Inventory your coverage**. Do you have employer-provided retiree insurance? If so, you may only need Part A.
2. **Plan for your gap years**. If you retire before 65, research your ACA options and estimate costs.
3. **Start Medicare planning early**. Begin exploring options 12 months before turning 65.
4. **Consult a Medicare expert**: Use trustworthy, free resources such as Medicare.gov.

Looking Ahead

We'll turn to Medicaid. It's often misunderstood, but essential for understanding long-term care funding. Even if you hope to never need it, knowing the rules can protect you and your family if life takes an unexpected turn. Understanding Medicaid's **look-back rules**, **asset limits**, and **estate recovery provisions** is essential, especially if you or your loved ones may need long-term care.

Don't assume health coverage is "handled" once you enroll in Medicare. There's more to protect. There's more to plan. And there's more at stake than many realize. Let's dig deeper next.

Medicare VS Long-term Care

Category	Medicare Coverage	Long-Term Care (LTC) Coverage
In-Home & Residential Care	Limited Home Health Aide (HHA) services	Full-time or part-time in-home care
	5 days of respite care (via hospice)	Extended respite care
	Hospice	Hospice (if part of LTC plan)
		Independent living
		Assisted living facility
		Memory care
	Limited skilled nursing (up to 100 days post-hospital stay)	Skilled nursing facility (beyond 100 days)
Medical Services (Part A & B)	Hospital care	—
	Doctor's services	—
	Inpatient surgery	—
	Outpatient surgery	—
	Physical therapy	—
	Medical equipment (e.g., walkers, hospital beds)	—
	Chemotherapy	—
Medicare Advantage (Part C)	Combines Part A, B, and often Part D	May include additional benefits (varies by plan)
	May offer dental and vision coverage	—
Prescription Drugs (Part D)	Prescription drug coverage	—
Cost Sharing	Deductibles	Varies based on private LTC policy
	Co-pays	Varies by provider and service
	Co-insurance	Varies by coverage level

CHAPTER EIGHT
Medicaid: Not a Welfare System

"When health is absent, wisdom cannot reveal itself, art cannot manifest, strength cannot fight, wealth becomes useless, and intelligence cannot be applied."

Herophilus

In the last chapter, we covered Medicare, the backbone of retirement healthcare for most Americans. For those who face long-term care needs, rising medical bills, or limited income and assets, Medicare may not be sufficient.

That's where **Medicaid** comes in.

If Medicare is a safety net, **Medicaid is the last line of defense.** And while it's often thought of as a "welfare" program, the truth is, many retirees, even those who were financially secure, end up needing it.

Understanding Medicaid early, **before a health crisis forces sudden decisions**, gives you the clarity to protect your assets, access the right care, and preserve your family's stability. Like a compass on a long journey, a proactive Medicaid plan helps you navigate toward care without losing your financial bearings.

In later chapters, especially on caregiving and after death, we'll explore what happens when Medicaid planning is delayed or ignored.

What Is Medicaid?

Medicaid is a joint federal and state program that provides healthcare coverage to eligible low-income individuals. Unlike Medicare, which is federally run, Medicaid is administered by individual states, meaning eligibility rules and benefits can vary significantly depending on where you live.

While Medicaid primarily covers healthcare costs for low-income populations, it's also the **largest single payer of long-term care** in the U.S. Planning ahead is essential if you think you or a loved one may need to access these benefits in the future.

Because Medicaid is state-run, it's important to consult your state's Medicaid office or a local elder law attorney to understand the specific rules where you live.

Why It Matters to You

Whether you're planning for yourself or aging parents, Medicaid is a **critical waypoint** on your aging and caregiving map. Without it, the road can quickly lead to depleted savings, family tension, and limited care options.

- **Medicare doesn't cover long-term care.** Medicaid does.
- **Long-term care is expensive.** Without a plan, it can wipe out a lifetime of savings.
- **Medicaid planning requires a five-year look-back.** Waiting until the crisis hits often limits your options.

As we'll explore more later, this matters not just financially, but emotionally and relationally.

Common Misconceptions

Myth: Medicaid is only for poor people. **Fact:** Many middle-class retirees qualify after asset restructuring or spending down.
Myth: I'll never need Medicaid. **Fact:** Over 60% of seniors will need long-term care at some point. Many end up relying on Medicaid to fund it.

Myth: I can give my assets away to qualify.
Fact: Medicaid has a five-year look-back period. Improper transfers can disqualify you or create a debt against your estate.

The 5-Year Look-Back Rule

One of the most important and misunderstood elements of Medicaid is the **five-year look-back period.**

When you apply, the state reviews **all financial transfers** made in the past 60 months. If you gifted assets, sold property for below market value, or transferred ownership, these could trigger a penalty period where you are **ineligible** for coverage.

To qualify, it's a bit like sitting at the poker table and being told you need to show every card in your hand, even the one hidden up your sleeve. You lay everything on the table, or you can't play the game. There's no bluffing this dealer either.

This is one of the biggest "clarity before crisis" moments in aging. If you misstep during the look-back period, you could face costly delays, out-of-pocket bills, or even the loss of your family home.

Your Medicaid compass points you toward lawful, timely asset moves that keep you eligible when care is needed. We'll explore this further in the discussion on estate planning, where proper documentation and titling can help avoid complications.

This lookback period is critical: incorrect planning can result in delayed eligibility or Medicaid debt owed by the estate.

Work with a qualified elder law attorney to properly and legally structure any asset transfer.

Eligibility Basics

To qualify for Medicaid, individuals must meet certain income and asset limits. The federal government sets baseline standards, but states have flexibility in how they apply them.

What Assets Are Counted?

Medicaid considers both **income** and **assets** when determining eligibility. While some assets are counted, others are exempt.

Commonly Exempt Assets: (These are the cards you get to hold through the game).

- Primary residence (with equity limits)
- Personal belongings and household items
- One vehicle
- Term life insurance
- Cash value life insurance (with minimal limits)
- Burial plot or prepaid funeral (with limits)
- Retirement accounts (if required minimum distributions are being made)

Community Spouse Resource Allowance (CSRA):

When one spouse needs care, and the other remains at home, the state protects a portion of the shared assets for the "community spouse." In many states, this amount is capped at around **$157,000** (as of 2025), though this varies.

We'll discuss more about protecting spousal resources and naming financial advocates when we discuss estate planning.

Age and Income Rules

Medicaid eligibility also depends on age, income, and disability status. Groups with unique eligibility criteria include:

- Children and pregnant women

- Adults aged 19–64 without dependents
- People age 65+
- Individuals who are blind or disabled (ABD category)

Income thresholds are tied to the **Federal Poverty Level (FPL)** and vary based on family size. Each state may have different thresholds or expansion programs under the Affordable Care Act (ACA).

What Medicaid Covers

Medicaid provides comprehensive health services, often including:

General Healthcare

- Doctor visits
- Hospital stays
- Prescription drugs
- Preventive care
- Transportation to medical appointments (varies by state)

Long-Term Care (LTC)

Medicaid is a primary payer for long-term care services in the U.S., including:

- **Institutional care**: nursing homes and assisted living (in some states)
- **Home- and community-based services (HCBS)**: help with daily activities, home care aides, and adult day services

Eligibility for long-term care benefits is stricter and requires both medical need and financial need. Again, planning early is essential.

Special Considerations

- **Dual Eligibility**: Some individuals qualify for both Medicare and Medicaid. These "dual eligibles" often receive more comprehensive coverage through coordinated or special plans called **D-SNPs (Dual Special Needs Plans)**.
- **Estate Recovery**: After the death of a Medicaid recipient, the state may seek to recover costs from the individual's estate. The right planning can **chart a path that shields your family from unnecessary loss** and preserves the legacy you've built.

Planning Strategies to Consider

The following strategies require legal and professional guidance, but may be appropriate if you are planning ahead:

- Irrevocable Medicaid Asset Protection Trusts
- Spending down assets strategically through home improvements or debt repayment
- Gifting assets early to family (well outside the look-back window)
- Transferring home title to a caregiver child or spouse (under certain exemptions)
- Annuities and income conversion tools to restructure assets

We'll expand on these in the estate planning chapter next, as many Medicaid planning strategies overlap with asset protection, legacy planning, and legal authority.

Success Story: Anil and Mira

Anil and Mira had spent decades building their estate. Between a family business, retirement savings, and real estate, they had accumulated more than most. As they entered their late seventies, one fear began to overshadow their sense of security: long-term care.

They had watched friends lose everything to nursing home bills. They had heard stories of families forced to sell homes and drain retirement accounts. Anil and Mira did not want their children and grandchildren to watch a lifetime of sacrifice vanish in just a few years of care expenses.

Rather than waiting for a crisis, they sought out an elder law attorney. Together, they walked through the realities of Medicaid's five-year look-back rule and how asset transfers could protect what mattered most. They weighed the tension every family faces: <u>is it more important to preserve a financial legacy for the next generation, or to keep every dollar available for our own potential care needs?</u>

After much discussion, they chose to prioritize their family. With the attorney's guidance, they established a Medicaid Asset Protection Trust and restructured ownership of certain properties. These moves were done early, well outside the look-back period, ensuring that when the time came, Medicaid would be an option without the fear of losing their estate overnight.

Anil and Mira understood that no plan is perfect, but their proactive approach gave them a sense of peace of mind. If one of them needed care, they had a pathway. If both remained healthy, their children and grandchildren would inherit the fruits of their work. Most importantly, they had clarity and the ability to live their later years without the constant shadow of "what if."

Clarity Affirmations

- Now I know Medicaid planning protects both dignity and assets.
- I can see how early planning reduces stress later.
- I understand why legal, financial, and healthcare advice must align.

- I will prepare for long-term care without leaving my family unprepared.

Action Plan

Here's your Medicaid navigation checklist: the steps that give you clarity now so you're not scrambling in crisis later.

1. **Identify your local Medicaid office.**
   Visit your state's health department website or use Medicaid.gov.
2. **Consult with an elder law attorney.**
   Especially important if you have complex assets, own real estate, or are concerned about care needs in the next five years.
3. **Start the conversation with family.**
   Involve adult children or Powers of Attorney early in the planning process to avoid confusion and delay.
4. **Document and organize.**
   Keep records of all major financial transactions. This simplifies the application and helps prevent issues during the look-back period.

Helpful Resources

- Medicaid.gov
- Benefits.gov Medicaid Eligibility Tool
- National Academy of Elder Law Attorneys (NAELA)
- Local Area Agencies on Aging (AAA)

Medicaid isn't just for the poor. It's an essential tool for aging with dignity, protecting your family, and preserving your legacy. With the right guidance, your Medicaid plan becomes a **true compass**, steering you away from last-minute decisions and toward a secure, intentional future.

Looking Ahead

We'll shift from healthcare to **estate planning**, where the legal tools you use today: Trusts, Wills, and Power of Attorney, determine how your assets are protected, who gets what, and how your legacy is carried out.

You'll see how poor Medicaid and estate planning often go hand in hand, and how proactive steps today can prevent chaos tomorrow.

Let's build that foundation together.

CHAPTER NINE

Estate Planning: Protect Your Legacy

"Planning is bringing the future into the present so that you can do something about it now."

Alan Lakein: *How to Get Control of Your Time and Your Life*

If you've followed the journey so far, from saving and spending habits to healthcare and Medicaid, this chapter is where it all converges. Estate planning is not simply about dividing money after you're gone. It's about clarity before crisis. It's the compass that points your family toward security, harmony, and purpose when life's storms arrive.

A well-designed estate plan gives your loved ones more than instructions; it gives them direction when they most need it. Without that guidance, families often face uncertainty, conflict, and costly delays, all while dealing with grief.

In earlier chapters, we saw how the absence of planning creates a void. Without clear decisions, assets stall in probate, medical choices spark disagreements, and even the strongest family bonds can fray. This chapter equips you with navigational tools to ensure your wishes are carried out, your loved ones are protected, and your legacy remains intact.

Here, we'll walk through the essential tools and concepts you need to plan your estate well, so your story can end with dignity and spare your loved ones unnecessary grief.

Later in the book, we'll explore the emotional fallout that can result from poor estate planning. This chapter lays the groundwork to avoid that outcome.

Three Goals

I emphasize the importance of estate planning because it accomplishes three important goals:

1. **Avoiding Probate:** This is the legal process of settling an estate in court. It's time-consuming, expensive, and public.
2. **Minimizing taxes and delays, saving time and money:** Proper planning can reduce or eliminate estate taxes, which is especially important for people with complex assets or a high net worth.
3. **Preserving relationships and intentions:** The right plan ensures your money, property, and possessions go to the right people at the right time, with less conflict and confusion.

Why This Matters Now

Estate planning often gets postponed because it forces us to face difficult topics, such as mortality, money, and family dynamics. It's easier to put off these hard conversations, but waiting invites chaos. This chaos affects our loved ones and us. In the absence of clear direction, assumptions take over, emotions boil, and relationships can be permanently damaged.

Clarity now is a gift. It relieves your loved ones from the burden of guessing, removes unnecessary legal battles, and ensures your wishes guide the journey rather than being lost in translation.

Author's Note: I've made every effort throughout this book to avoid overly technical jargon, but in this chapter, legal terminology is essential. Where needed, I will explain these terms in plain language to make this important topic as straightforward as possible.

Key term: Probate. The legal process for settling assets.

We want to avoid it. Think probation. Like going to the DMV, long lines, lots of paperwork, and sad people. It's also quite expensive.

From Combat to Conflict: A Personal Story

In combat, the threats I worried about were visible: IEDs, small arms fire, and RPGs. In estate planning, the threats are quieter: family conflict, probate delays, and unintended tax burdens. And just like in combat, preparation makes all the difference.

Let me tell you a story, not about a client, but about my own grandmother.

A Family's Turning Point

She lived close to most of her eight children. My dad died of brain cancer at 33. This is when my thoughts on legacy really began. When you lose someone, you learn how important your time together is, which led me to become closer to that family than I ever imagined. Our family's main gathering spot was her cottage, situated on the shores of Baptist Lake, known in our family as "The Mighty Baptist" (ironically, for a family of Catholics).

That cottage was the backdrop for so many memories: summer days taking out the old Jon boat to look for turtles in the cove, turning the pontoon into a party barge for the boat parade, tubing behind my uncle's boats, and narrowly avoiding pyrotechnic disaster every Fourth of July. I even wrote a school essay about how much I loved it.

After my grandpa passed, Grandma still wasn't "alone," not with our ever-growing crew of children, grandchildren, and great-grandchildren. I was lucky to grow remarkably close to her. We'd "get lost" together on the way to garage sales and flea markets, then watch *The Lawrence Welk Show* while catching up as she drank her "evening tea." She always wanted to know what was *really* going on in my life, not just the surface stuff. My other grandparents weren't like that, like a friend. Now, as a dad, I see how valuable that connection is. It's something I'm intentional about with my kids and their grandparents.

We became so close that I took her to the Bahamas right after high school, before shipping off to the Army. How many people get to say they took their grandma on a tropical vacation? After I returned from the war, I stayed at her place the summer before college started. It became a place of healing. She was a safe person to process life with, a gentle listener. College was just 20 minutes away, so we became regulars at the cottage. Even after I moved to Chicago, we visited whenever we could. From my perspective, she was perfect, the glue that held us all together.

Of course, no family is perfect. In big families, there's always some history and drama. Sometimes you put on a smile so everyone can get along. But over time, resentments, misunderstandings, and strong opinions can build, especially when hard conversations are avoided.

As Grandma got older, that tension started to show. A hard fall didn't cause the family stress, but it accelerated it. Yes, there were meetings and efforts to plan, but the emotional undercurrents remained. Decisions about her housing, finances, caregiving, and independence became harder and more divisive.

When she passed, the years of tension finally snapped. People chose sides, and some relationships never recovered. Disagreements turned into divisions. The cottage was sold. The family no longer gathers like it once did. The traditions, the holiday get-togethers, the legacy tied to that place, gone.

Not because anyone was selfish. Everyone wanted what was best for Grandma. But without a clear, shared plan and without intentional communication, we all lost something.

Her story reminds me that estate planning is about more than titles, deeds, and account balances. It's about protecting what truly matters: your people, your peace, and the places that hold your history.

This chapter isn't about who's right or wrong. It's about what you can do differently.

The Big Picture: What Is Estate Planning?

Think of your estate plan as your directional guide for:

- **Wealth** – Who gets what, and when.
- **Care** – Who makes decisions if you can't.
- **Harmony** – How to avoid conflict and preserve relationships.

At its core, estate planning answers three key questions:

- What do you own?
- Who gets what?
- Who's in charge?

3 Core Benefits of Estate Planning

Financial

- **Asset Direction** – Control where your assets go.
- **Tax Efficiency** – Reduce or eliminate estate tax.
- **Liquidity** – Ensure cash is available for final expenses.

Personal

- **Family Harmony** – Clear instructions reduce conflict.
- **Generational Support** – Plan for children and grandchildren.
- **Charitable Giving** – Leave a legacy to causes you value.
- **Guardianship & Care** – Appoint caretakers or medical advocates.
- **Home Protection** – Keep the family home in the family.

Functional

- **Avoid Probate** – Save time, money, and keep your affairs private.

- **Fiduciary Control** – Choose who manages your estate.
- **Conservator Planning** – Assign someone to manage finances if needed.

2 Stages of Estate Planning

1. The Living Estate

Covers your care and assets while you're alive.

Key legal tools:

- **General Power of Attorney (POA)** – Handles finances and legal matters if you lose the capacity to handle them yourself.
- **Medical Power of Attorney (POA)** – Makes health decisions if you can't.
- **Living Will** – States your end-of-life medical wishes.
- **Living Trust** – Directs financial assets (can avoid probate).
- **Guardianship & Conservatorship** – For dependents or incapacitated adults.
- **Prenuptial/Post-nuptial Agreements** – Define asset ownership in marriage.
- **Funeral Representative Designation** – Specifies who handles your final arrangements.

These documents are especially important if you anticipate medical decline, have dependent children or adults, or want to ease burdens on your spouse. This theme continues as we discuss caregiving and end-of-life planning.

2. The Legacy Estate

Deals with how your assets are distributed after death.

Key legal tools:

- **Will** – Directs specific assets and appoints guardians.

- **Revocable Trust** – Avoids probate, allows control while living.
- **Irrevocable Trust** – Removes assets from estate (estate tax planning).
- **Testamentary Trust** – Activated at death.
- **Lady Bird Deed** – Transfers real estate outside of probate.
- **Beneficiary Designations & Titling** – Direct transfers without probate.
- **Pour-Over Will** – Moves any unlisted assets into your trust.

Each of these tools serves a different function. Used properly, they ensure a smooth transition. Used improperly, or not at all, they can leave a mess.

6 Celebrities with Complicated Estates

You didn't know my grandma, but these names are probably much more familiar. Note: even the rich and famous don't always thoughtfully plan for the protection and transfer of their own wealth.

- Michael Jackson-$500 million debate over the Will and execution of the Will
- Prince-$300 million died without a Will, multiple claimants
- Robin Williams $100 million contested Will between wife and children
- Whitney Houston $20 million after daughter died, contested between mother, siblings, and boyfriend
- Heath Ledger $20 million estate contested between parents, sisters, daughter, and the mother of the daughter

Contrast that with the **Walton family** (Walmart), who used over 30 trusts to strategically and smoothly transition billions.

Special Situations That Require an Attorney

- Multiple properties or businesses across states or countries
- Ownership of farmland, art, collectibles, or private stock
- Gifting to grandchildren or foreign beneficiaries
- Unmarried partnerships or significant age differences between spouses
- Estates exceeding the federal exemption ($13.99M in 2025).
- Having **no spouse or no kids**. If there is no clearly defined heir or beneficiary, this gets complex quickly.

If any of these apply, consult with an **estate planning attorney**, preferably one who understands **Medicaid integration**, tax planning, and family governance.

Common Misconceptions

Myth: A Will avoids probate. **Fact:** A Will guides probate; it doesn't avoid it.
Myth: Beneficiaries get everything tax-free. **Fact:** Inheritance may be tax-free to the beneficiary, but the estate may owe taxes. See the section about inherited retirement accounts.
Myth: A Trust avoids all taxes. **Fact:** Revocable trusts avoid probate, not taxes. Proper structuring is key.
Myth: I don't need a lawyer; I'll just use online forms. **Fact:** DIY documents can be challenged or ineffective. Legal guidance is worth the investment.

Online forms can be a convenient way to create a "vanilla" estate plan. They're quick, inexpensive, and handle simple beneficiary designations, but where they often fall short is in

scenario planning. Good attorneys ask *what happens next* when life takes an unexpected turn. They've seen it all, so they can help you plan for the 5th domino falling.

For example:

- You name your daughter as your sole beneficiary. She inherits everything.
- When she later passes away, her estate (including what she inherited from you) goes to her spouse, your son-in-law, not directly to your grandchildren.
- If your son-in-law remarries and becomes part of a blended family, your legacy could unintentionally benefit a new spouse or stepchildren instead of staying in your bloodline.

This is why thoughtful estate planning goes beyond just naming beneficiaries. It anticipates contingencies and puts protections in place to ensure your wishes are carried out across generations.

Myth: I'm not wealthy enough to need an estate plan. **Fact:** If you own a home, have kids, or care about who gets what, you need one.
Myth: I already have a Will, so I'm covered. **Fact:** Wills don't avoid probate. Only properly titled assets or trusts do.
Myth: My family will figure it out. **Fact:** Families often fracture under stress. Planning is a gift, not a burden.
Myth: I'll do it later. **Fact:** Later often becomes never. The best time is now.

How Probate Works, and How to Avoid It

Probate is the court process for settling an estate. It's public, slow, and costly. It's triggered when assets aren't titled correctly or lack a proper beneficiary.

Key risks that trigger probate:

- Dying without a Will (intestate)
- Owning property in multiple states
- Outdated or contested Wills

Steps in Probate

1. The will is located and verified
2. A personal representative is appointed (usually the executor if there is a Will
3. Probate bonds are posted
4. Assets are inventoried and appraised
5. Creditors are notified and paid
6. Taxes are filed
7. Remaining assets are distributed

Ways to Avoid Probate:

- Use **Trusts** with updated documents and Pour-Over Wills.
- Name **beneficiaries** (not "estate") on accounts and policies.
- **Title assets** properly (avoid Tenants in Common).

Comparing Key Roles in Care and Estate Management

When families plan for aging, illness, or passing, several legal and practical roles may come into play. Each has specific responsibilities and limitations. Understanding the distinctions helps prevent confusion and ensures that duties are assigned wisely.

Caregiver (not a formal role with legal authority)

A caretaker provides hands-on, day-to-day assistance.

- Driving to appointments
- Cleaning and maintaining the home
- Helping with bathing and personal care
- Managing the landscaping
- Hiring outside help when needed

Healthcare Power of Attorney (POA)

This person makes **medical decisions** on your behalf if you cannot.

- Approving or denying medical treatments
- Making decisions about DNR (Do Not Resuscitate) orders
- Authorizing or refusing life support
- Managing medication choices
- Consenting to or declining surgical procedures

General Power of Attorney (Durable or Non-Durable)

This role covers **financial and legal matters.**

- Paying bills
- Updating contact or account information
- Managing leases, contracts, or other legal documents
- Important limitation: **cannot create or change a Will**
- Important limitation: **cannot make medical decisions**

Personal Representative (Executor)

The personal representative manages affairs after someone's death.

- Filing the final income tax return
- Selecting and working with a probate attorney
- Distributing personal items according to the Will
- Administering and settling the estate
- Must follow the exact terms of the Will

Trustee

A trustee manages assets placed into a Trust.

- Investing funds responsibly
- Distributing funds as directed in the trust
- Following the exact terms of the trust document

You're the Trustee or Personal Rep. Now What?

It's an honor to be named, but also a heavy burden, especially if you're grieving. I dive deep into this in the chapter on planning in grief and after death.

Tips:

- Know your limits. It's okay to get help.
- Don't try to do everything alone.
- Consider working with a **corporate trustee or estate administrator.**

These professionals help with:

- Settling accounts

- Filing taxes
- Managing assets
- Reducing conflict

Handling the Home

Three common ways to handle real estate:

1. **Lady Bird Deed** – Transfers home on death while keeping control.
2. **Qualified Personal Residence Trust** – Allows the spouse to stay, passing the home to the children.
3. **Joint Tenancy with Rights of Survivorship (JTWROS)** – Transfers to co-owner on death.

Ask:

- Will the home stay in the family?
- Will your loved ones be able to live there?
- What's the tax impact?

Final Expenses: Ensuring Liquidity

Expenses at death include funeral costs, medical bills, legal fees, and taxes. You'll need accessible cash.

Options:

1. **Prepay Funeral Costs** – Lock in today's prices, but it may not be transferable.
2. **Final Expense Insurance** – Small life insurance policies ($10–20k).
3. **Self-Fund** – Use designated assets in your estate plan.

Fraud and Abuse: Crossing the Line

We will dive deep into relationship dynamics and the complexities of families, and the impact of those we hold closest. Most of the time, the abuser isn't a stranger. It's someone within the family circle. That's why family conflict can't just be brushed off as "drama." When money, power, and stress collide, sometimes it's not just about dignity, but it's about survival.

Example from Real Life

I once worked with a woman who held Power of Attorney for her father. Her brother actively undermined her by withholding medications, hoping their father would die so he could expedite an inheritance. The father knew it was happening but couldn't bring himself to admit that his own son was capable of such a thing.

Together, we talked through the impossible choices. Should she pursue a restraining order, knowing it would shatter what was left of the family dynamic? Should she give up the POA if she didn't have the power to enforce it? And hanging over it all was the terrifying reality: if her father died under her watch because of abuse or neglect, *she* could be held legally responsible.

Can you imagine being in this position? You're legally bound to protect someone's life, while your own sibling is gambling with that life for money. Do you file charges for elder abuse? Do you get involved with the courts and risk destroying the family forever? Or do you turn a blind eye and live with the guilt?

This is what elderly abuse can look like. It isn't always a stranger or a scammer. Sometimes, it's the people sitting across from you at the same holiday table.

Types of Fraud and Abuse Families Should Watch For

Whether you're taking care of yourself or someone else, being aware of these dangers can help protect you and your family.

1. Financial Exploitation

- **Romance scams**: A predator preys on a widow or widower, builds a "relationship," then slowly asks for money, gains access to accounts, or even gets named as Power of Attorney.
- **Fraud and theft**: Falsifying documents, stealing banking information, draining credit cards, or walking off with cash and family heirlooms.
- **Real estate exploitation**: Pressuring someone to sign over a deed or transfer property.
- **Investment scams**: Fake businesses, annuities, or "can't miss" opportunities.
- **Phishing and tech scams**: IRS calls, "your grandchild is in jail," fake tech support, and other cons.
- **Medical fraud**: Billing for services never provided or stealing prescription drugs.

2. Physical and Emotional Abuse

- **Intentional abuse**: Starving the person needing care, withholding medications, letting them freeze, leaving them in soiled clothing, physical abuse, or deliberately avoiding medical care.
- **Emotional abuse**: Isolation, threats, or shame. *"If you don't sign this, I won't take you to the doctor."*
- **Institutional neglect**: Facilities leaving residents with bedsores, infections, or untreated injuries.

3. Manipulation and Control

- **Undue influence**: Manipulating Mom or Dad into changing a Will or Trust.

- **Predatory caregivers or "friends"**: Paid helpers, neighbors, or acquaintances who isolate and exploit the vulnerable person.

If you suspect these are happening, consult with an elder law attorney.

Summary

Estate planning is your compass when life shifts unexpectedly. Done well, it not only directs your assets but also preserves your family's dignity, strengthens their connection, and ensures your legacy survives intact.

The best time to set your course is before the storm, while you have the clarity to lead, the time to prepare, and the power to choose.

While this chapter gives you a solid foundation, working with a skilled estate planning attorney is the best way to tailor a plan to your unique circumstances. Your legacy deserves it.

Clarity Affirmations

- Now I know estate planning is about people, not just documents.
- I can see how Wills, Trusts, and Powers of Attorney provide clarity.
- I understand that an estate plan protects both assets and relationships.
- I will begin building a legacy that lasts.

Action Plan

1. **Inventory your assets.**
   List everything you own, who owns it, and how it's titled.

2. **Review your beneficiaries.**
   Retirement accounts and insurance policies should match your current wishes.

3. **Create or update your estate documents.**
   Work with a qualified attorney, especially if your life or financial situation has changed.

4. **Talk to your family.**
   Be clear about your wishes. Prevent conflict through communication, not assumptions.

Looking Ahead

We'll talk about **charitable giving**, not just as a tax strategy, but as a way to express your values and leave a living legacy. Then we return to the emotional weight of care, where aging parents, legal responsibility, and family dynamics collide.

The plan you make here gives you more than control over assets. It gives your loved ones guidance, comfort, and a restful hope. We'll also navigate relationship and family dynamics to tie it all together.

CHAPTER TEN

Charitable Giving: Leaving a Legacy That Lasts

"The measure of a life is not its duration but its donation."

Corrie Ten Boom

Once we've charted a course for income, lifestyle, health care, and legacy, one of my favorite conversations begins: giving.

Charitable giving isn't just for the wealthy. It's a tool available to anyone who wants to make an impact, whether through their time, talents, or treasure.

Just like with retirement planning, you don't flip a switch at age 65 and suddenly become generous. Giving is a habit, a mindset, and often a reflection of your deepest values. We explored what "true wealth" means. Here, we readdress that question: **What are you leaving behind, and who does it benefit?**

Much like estate planning, charitable giving can range from simple to overly complex. Some strategies can be implemented directly; others require a team, an advisor, an attorney, and a tax professional to ensure it's done right.

When I work with clients, we start by exploring their vision for giving. Next, we identify strategies to align with that vision. Finally, we partner with other professionals to help structure the plan, ensuring tax efficiency and legal compliance.

Start with Questions, Not Dollars

Effective giving starts with thoughtfulness, not cash.

- How do you want to be remembered?

- What causes or people shaped your life?
- Where do you feel called to give back?
- Is your focus church, college, children, or charity?

In our planning meetings, I always ask clients to define their vision for giving. It's not just about money, it's about purpose.

Later chapters will dive into how to carry these values through caregiving, family dynamics, and after-death planning. It starts here, in the present, with your intention.

The Emotional Benefit of Giving

There's a unique satisfaction that comes from giving while living, because you can still see the difference it makes and guide it with your own hands. Think of these as points on your generosity compass with different directions you can take to express your values. Research shows that people who give regularly experience:

- Greater life satisfaction
- Lower depression and anxiety
- Stronger social bonds

Whether through time, mentorship, or money, giving is one of the most powerful antidotes to isolation, a theme we revisit in the caregiving and retirement lifestyle chapters.

What Counts as Charitable Giving?

Giving isn't limited to writing a check to a 501(c)(3). It can include:

- Volunteering time or skills
- Donating appreciated stock or real estate
- Creating scholarships or memorial funds

- Establishing donor-advised funds (DAFs)
- Supporting ministries or local families in need
- Naming a charity in your estate plan

We'll explore advanced strategies that reduce taxes while increasing impact, such as qualified charitable distributions (QCDs) and charitable trusts.

These strategies are like navigational markers, helping you avoid tax pitfalls and steer resources toward the causes that matter most.

But first, let's cover the basics.

Key Giving Limits (2025)

Author's Note: These limits are current under the 2017 Tax Cuts and Jobs Act. Always confirm with a qualified tax professional before acting.

- **$19,000** – Annual gift exclusion per recipient. You can give up to this amount without using your lifetime exemption or filing a gift tax return.
- **$38,000** – Married couples can "split" gifts, doubling the exclusion. If you split gifts, you must report it, but there's no tax if you stay under the combined limit.
- **$13,990,000** – Federal estate tax exemption (per person). Anything above this may be subject to federal taxation. **This increases to $15 million in 2026.**
- **$95,000** – Maximum "super-funding" of a 529 education savings plan (5 years' worth of gifts at once).
- **Unlimited** – Transfers between U.S. citizen spouses are exempt from gift tax.
- **$190,000** – Annual gift limit to a non-citizen spouse.

- **$108,000** – Maximum Qualified Charitable Distribution (QCD) per year, per person from an IRA if over age 70½. These donations go directly to a charity and **do not count as taxable income**. **This means a married couple that qualifies could give $216,000 combined.**
- **60% of AGI:** The maximum cash charitable deduction allowed when itemizing.

Special Gifting Exceptions (Non-Taxable)

Some gifts don't count toward the annual or lifetime limits if made **directly** to an institution:

- **Tuition payments** – Pay directly to the school (e.g., your granddaughter's tuition at Georgia Tech), and no gift tax applies.
    - Keep in mind, this is for **tuition** only. Room and board, equipment, and supplies are not included. An advisor can help you explore other ways to fund those items.
- **Medical expenses** – Pay the hospital or provider directly for a loved one's care, and it's excluded from gift limits. If you pay the one receiving care, there is no tax benefit.

Ways to Give

For Tax Planning:

- **Direct Gift** – Simple transfers to individuals or organizations. Rules vary for public vs. private entities.
- **Donor-Advised Fund (DAF)** – A flexible tool: you receive a tax deduction when funding the DAF and later decide where to direct the funds. Think of a DAF as a "charity checking account." You donate cash or appreciated assets to the fund,

take the tax deduction that year, and decide later where to send the money.

- Immediate tax deduction
- Flexibility in timing gifts
- Anonymity (if desired)
- Simpler record-keeping
- DAFs are ideal for years with high income, a business sale, or inheritance. Business owners, take a look at the chapter dedicated to you.

- **Qualified Charitable Distribution (QCD)** – If you're age 70½ or older, you can give directly from your IRA to a qualified charity. It counts toward your Required Minimum Distribution (RMD) but is **not** taxable income.

Note: QCDs cannot be used for Donor-Advised Funds or private foundations.

- **Private Foundation** – Offers full control and long-term planning but comes with complex rules and higher costs. Best for larger estates or families wanting to establish a formal giving structure.
- **Qualified Personal Residence Trust (QPRT)** – Transfers your home to a trust. You retain the right to live there for a set time. After that, the home passes to your heirs, reducing estate taxes while excluding appreciation from your taxable estate.

For Income Generation (and a tax break at the time of the gift):

- **Charitable Gift Annuity (CGA)** – You donate to a charity and receive a fixed income stream for life. At death, the remainder benefits the charity.

- **Charitable Lead Trust (CLT)** – You fund a trust that pays income to a charity for a set period. Afterward, the remaining assets return to you or your heirs.
- **Charitable Remainder Trust (CRT)** – You receive income for life (or a set term), and the remainder goes to charity upon death.

The Family Conversation

One of the most powerful outcomes of charitable giving is the example it sets for your family.

- If your children inherit everything, will they carry on your values?
- Have you told them why giving is important to you?
- Are there causes they care about that could be funded in your honor?
- Do you want to involve them in your giving decisions?

These conversations are especially helpful if you plan to give unequally or outside the family. Clear communication prevents resentment and confusion.

We'll explore this dynamic further soon.

Living Generously

True generosity isn't measured in dollars; it's measured in freedom, time, and willingness. Many of my favorite stories come from clients who gave when they didn't "have to" and were better off for it. As a member of my local Rotary club, giving and service are at the center. Seeing the impact of your generosity is awe-inspiring. If you're looking for community, ways to get involved, and ways to give, check out your local clubs.

Generosity reflects what you value. It doesn't reduce your wealth. It multiplies it in ways you can't always count.

Clarity Affirmations

- Now I know giving is about meaning, not just money.
- I can align my generosity with my values.
- I understand the tools that can make my giving last.
- I will leave a legacy that reflects who I am.

Action Plan

Don't wait for "someday." Someday is when the crisis has already arrived. Small acts now, guided by a clear plan, can change lives and protect the legacy you want to leave.

1. **Clarify your giving goals.**
   What causes matter most to you? What impact do you want to leave?

2. **Update your estate plan.**
   Include charitable bequests or Trusts in your Will or Living Trust.

3. **Explore tax-efficient giving.**
   Consider QCDs, donor-advised funds, or appreciated stock donations.

4. **Talk to your family.**
   Share your heart for giving and involve them if appropriate.

5. **Give now**
   Don't wait for "someday." Small acts now can change lives.

Meet with your financial advisor to define your giving goals. From there, bring in a tax expert and estate attorney to identify the right vehicles and ensure proper implementation.

You've spent a lifetime building wealth. Now is your chance to use it for good, for family, for community, and for the values you want to carry forward.

Charitable giving is one form of legacy, one direction on your life's compass. How we care for one another, especially in seasons of need, is another.

Looking Ahead

We pivot to one of the most emotionally charged and financially complex realities of aging: **caregiving and extended care**. This is where preparation meets real life, where health, relationships, and financial responsibility collide.

Let's talk about what happens when the care falls on your shoulders, or when you're the one who needs it.

Part 3: Care, Conflict, and Legacy

CHAPTER ELEVEN
Senior Care: Caregiving and Extended Care

"To care for those who once cared for us is one of the highest honors."

Tia Walker

Few topics are more personal or more complicated than caregiving. When someone you love becomes dependent, everything changes. Roles shift, emotions rise, and money matters become messy. Often, amidst these fluctuations, there's no clear plan. Without a compass to guide you, it's easy to lose your way in the emotional, financial, and logistical storms that follow.

In caregiving, there are moments of decision that shape everything that follows. You either prepare before the storm, or you scramble when it hits. Preventive planning and communication create clarity; reactive planning creates crisis.

This chapter will have three parts: the caregiver's perspective, the perspective of the one receiving care, and the tools that tie it all together.

I'll blend the costs, relationships, responsibility, and realities of aging and caregiving. It connects directly to the legal tools of estate planning, the health systems of Medicare and Medicaid, and the emotional weight of legacy and family conflict. Discussing your own care and the loss of independence can be difficult, so you may want to avoid it. If you do that, it's like avoiding the dentist: the longer you put it off, the worse it gets. This is actually worse, because your family will deal with what you avoided.

Career and Family

You met Mark earlier when we introduced him as he opened his home to his aging mother. We saw the impact on his career and family. By default, he became the Power of Attorney, care manager, household administrator, family financier, grief counselor, and estate executor. At every turn, he felt unsure. Was he doing the right thing? Would his siblings accuse him of overstepping? Could he afford this sacrifice?

Mark ended up finding a team of pros and putting a plan in place, so his family could navigate the present and their future.

This chapter is about how to put a caregiving compass in place early, so your loved ones have clear direction instead of heavy uncertainty.

Triggers: When Caregiving Begins

Caregiving doesn't begin at a certain age; it begins at a moment. A person becomes a caregiver the instant their loved one can no longer manage fully on their own. That shift can be triggered by:

- An accident or fall that suddenly changes mobility or independence.
- A diagnosis that alters daily function or long-term outlook.
- A combination of symptoms that, together, prevent a loved one from living with full independence.

These moments rarely come with warning, which is why preparing early matters.

Part I: The Caregiver's Burden

What Is Caregiving?

In the U.S., over **53 million** adults are unpaid caregivers. Most are untrained formally. Many are exhausted, and nearly all are navigating a system they didn't prepare for. **Caregiving** refers to any support, medical, emotional, logistical, or financial, provided to someone who can no longer manage independently.

It often starts subtly:

- **Home Maintenance:** Cleaning, cooking, transportation.
- **Medical Support:** Managing meds, appointments, coordination.
- **Companionship:** Reading, entertainment, outings.
- Offering basic tech support. If you can help your loved one understand a mouse, window, and how to put pictures on Facebook, or get on a FaceTime call, you're doing great.

Then over time, it expands:

- **Personal Hygiene:** Bathing, toileting, grooming.
- **Full-time supervision:** Round-the-clock care. Alarms, medication reminders, and residency changes
- **Financial Management:** Paying bills, managing accounts (with POA).
- **End-of-life support:** You've been there from the beginning, and now through the end, and everything that goes with it.

Two Challenges

Being a caregiver to an aging parent or loved one is often described as both an honor and a burden. It's emotionally and physically demanding, sometimes thankless, and almost always more complex than it appears on the surface.

Challenge 1: You may feel financially unprepared.

According to AARP, the average family caregiver spends **$7,242 per year** in unreimbursed costs. That's before you factor in lost wages or health effects. If you consider that many families already carry significant debt and don't have enough cash on hand to cover a basic emergency, you understand how devastating this can be. Ramsey

Solutions claims the average credit card balance for someone in the U.S. is over $6,000. Can you really afford another financial burden?

We can calculate the financial aspect closely, but some costs are not so clear. These costs are often hidden because they accumulate slowly. Without planning, they can steer your life off course before you realize how far you've drifted.

Challenge 2: You may feel technically, physically, or emotionally unprepared.

- **Career**
    - Job creep is common as care expands beyond initial expectations.
    - Missing work, losing out on a well-deserved promotion, or quitting your job entirely
- **Health**
    - Seeing your own health deplete under stress, lack of sleep, and building anxiety, and even depression
    - Burnout from long-term responsibility.
- **Relationships:**
    - Marital tension, sibling conflict, social isolation
    - Telling your kids that you can't go on the family vacation anymore
    - Having another fight with your spouse, kids, or siblings, who don't understand the pressure you're under
    - Guilt: Asking for help can feel like failure.
    - Resistance: Aging parents may reject help or resent loss of independence.

- **Finances**
    - Out-of-pocket expenses, missed contributions to savings
- **Time**
    - You miss date nights, events with kids or grandkids, tell your friends "No, you can't visit," cancel the vacation…

Those are some serious costs.

Questions to consider before becoming a caregiver:

- Do I have the time, energy, and physical ability?
- How will this affect my marriage, career, finances, or mental health?
- Will it strain family relationships, especially with siblings, your spouse, or your kids?

Case Study: The Caregiver's Journey

Let me introduce you to Steve and Linda, active in their 50s, enjoying the freedom of an empty nest and serving faithfully in their church. Life was full, balanced, and moving along with purpose.

Then Linda's parents, Harold and Ruth, began to decline in health. Like many adult children, Linda gradually stepped into a caregiving role. While she had siblings both nearby and across the country, Linda became the primary point of contact and support.

When I asked Linda if she had prepared a formal care plan, she said she hadn't. In the beginning, it didn't seem necessary. It started with small tasks, giving rides, helping with groceries, nothing that significantly disrupted their lifestyle or daily routine.

Caregiving has a way of creeping in quietly before it takes over completely. What began as occasional errands slowly evolved into a full-time commitment: managing 13 medications a day, attending frequent hospital visits, and providing round-the-clock care. The conditions were complex: dementia, brain tumors, and mini-strokes, and the emotional and physical demands were intense.

When Harold passed in 2019, the weight of those years was deeply felt. By then, Steve had experienced a heart attack, and Linda had poured years of her life into caregiving. While other family members may have contributed in separate ways or simply been limited by circumstance, the reality is that long-term caregiving often falls disproportionately on one person.

They gave up vacations, privacy, and peace, not out of obligation, but out of love. A shared plan could have set clear expectations, preserved their health and marriage, and ensured other family members were part of the journey. Without it, love alone had to carry the weight, and it nearly broke them.

KEY DECISION POINT: When caregiving begins to creep in, will you acknowledge it early, or wait until it becomes overwhelming?

What could have helped?

1. Family meetings, open communication about expectations and responsibilities.
2. A clear, updated Will, to minimize conflict and clarify wishes.
3. Durable Medical and General Powers of Attorney, for timely decisions.
4. Realistic conversations about the impact caregiving has on the caregiver's own life and goals.

Special Note for the Sandwich Generation: When You Are Both the Child and the Caregiver

Many readers find themselves managing their parents' aging process while raising children or planning their own retirement. You are grieving the slow loss of a parent, while also trying to parent, provide, and plan. And all the while, your role as a *child* gets blurred.

The emotional toll is heavy. Grief creeps in as you watch someone you love slowly fade, even while they're still here. Frustration builds when you feel isolated or unsupported by siblings. Somewhere along the way, many caregivers lose a piece of themselves by sacrificing their own goals, identity, and rest.

The practical challenges stack on top of that emotional weight. Many caregivers cut back on work or dip into their own pockets to cover expenses. Navigating the maze of healthcare, insurance, and legal documents can feel overwhelming and mind-numbing.

So, what helps? Sometimes it means hiring professional caretakers or bringing in outside support. Sometimes it's leaning on an estate planning attorney to set up clear Powers of Attorney or using a corporate trustee to avoid family conflict. Often, it's looking ahead and using your current caregiving experience to shape your own aging plan, so your children won't carry the same burden.

Even with help, caregivers still need strategies to protect themselves. That might mean seeking support from family, friends, or a caregiving group. It means setting boundaries and saying no when the cost to yourself is too high. It means prioritizing rest and accepting respite care when you need it because burnout helps no one.

Caregiving can bring out the best in families, but it can also expose the cracks that were always there. Which path yours takes depends on planning, communication, and empathy.

Download the **Caregiver Guide** from my website to develop your own plan.

Preventative Steps for Aging Parents or Spouses

If your loved one is aging, the best gift you can give them, and yourself, is a plan.

1. **Open the conversation**
   Ask what they want. Where do they want to live? Who do they trust to manage things? You can find all the details for this conversation in the **Personal Care Guide online.**

2. **Organize legal documents**
   Review POAs, Wills, and medical directives.

3. **List their resources**
   Income sources, assets, insurance policies, pensions, and Medicaid eligibility.

4. **Visit facilities early**
   Don't wait until a crisis. Tour places while your parents are still well enough to choose. Their compass should guide them, not the clock.

5. **Document everything**
   Keep records of care decisions, spending, and legal updates. This protects everyone involved.

When you do this, what does clarity look like?

- The family meeting to gain direction and support
- A personal care plan for respite and self-care
- Knowing your loved ones' wishes are being honored, and watching them live in dignity
- A caregiving budget that reviews insurance, savings, and assets well before the first bill is due

- Knowing your loved one feels at home, no matter where they end up staying

Caregiving isn't a one-sided story. For every overwhelmed and heartbroken caregiver, a parent or spouse is wrestling with loss of independence and dignity. The things we take for granted every day, like being able to go where we want, feed ourselves, bathe ourselves, and take care of our homes, are privileges for the young and healthy.

Part II Receiving Care

The unprepared:

- Assumes their family understands their wishes
- Believes their children can "handle it" or "figure it out"
- Places the burden of their care on the family members
- Avoids the signs that their health is in decline

The planner:

- Developed a care team, so no one is overwhelmed
- Knows where they will call home, even if circumstances change
- Allocates funds for their care
- Communicates their care and legacy goals
- Does their best to align their family

Planning for Your Own Care

It's not just about aging parents or spouses. You must also prepare for your own future.

Ask yourself:

- Who will take care of me if I'm no longer independent?
- Do I want to age in place or move?
- Will I burden my children?
- How will I pay for care?

Answers to these questions shape:

- Your long-term care insurance decision
- Your home modifications
- Your estate and Medicaid plan
- Your family conversations

5 Key Questions for Care Planning

1. **Where do I want to receive care?**
   At home? With children? In a professional support environment?
2. **Who will make decisions for me?**
   Medical POA, financial POA, and successor trustees.
3. **How will care be funded?**
   Savings, insurance, VA benefits, Medicaid?
4. **What kind of care do I want and not want?**
   Clarify in your Living Will or advanced directive.
5. **Does my family know my plan?**
   Unspoken plans often become misunderstood ones.

KEY DECISION POINT: Will you tell your family your wishes while you can, or assume they'll just figure it out?

1. Have you ever been a caregiver? What did it teach you (time, money, stress)?
2. Do you expect to need care someday? What signs would trigger planning?
3. Where do you prefer to receive care? At home, with family, or in a care community?
4. Who will make decisions if you can't (Medical POA, Financial POA, successor trustee, backups)?
5. How will care be funded (savings, insurance/LTC rider, VA benefits, Medicaid)?
6. What care do you want and not want? Capture it in your advance directive/Living Will.
7. Which legal documents are in place and current (POAs, Will/Trust, HIPAA release, beneficiaries, letter of instruction)?
8. What is the family caregiving plan? Who does what, boundaries, respite, paid help?
9. Will your children (or others) be involved and how, specifically?
10. Does your family know the plan and where documents are stored? (Unspoken plans become misunderstood ones.)

Part III Care Resources

<u>Special Note on Alzheimer's & Dementia</u>

There are days when the person you love looks at you like a kind stranger. Names slip away. Stories repeat. Moods turn without warning. Personalities stretch and change until the familiar feels far away. For spouses and caregivers, Alzheimer's and other dementias can feel like a rollercoaster you never chose to ride, hope and heartbreak in the same afternoon.

If that's where you are, this section is for you. You are not weak for feeling tired, angry, or sad. You are not failing. You are carrying something heavy.

What follows won't diagnose or treat; it will help you organize what to ask, what to document, and whom to call. Dementia raises challenging questions about **capacity**, **consent**, and **safety**. The most loving next step is often to work with specialists: medical, legal, and care-coordination, who work in this world every day. Use the tools in this book to start the right conversations, then let experts tailor a plan for your family. You do not have to do this alone.

Alzheimer's and other dementias change **how** decisions are made. This book and its guides can help you organize questions, prepare documents, and start family conversations. Still, they are **not** medical, legal, or tax advice, and they are **not** a substitute for personalized care planning.

Capacity & Consent

Decision-making capacity can fluctuate and is task-specific. If there is **any** doubt about capacity, pause DIY changes and consult qualified professionals (medical and legal). Documents signed without sufficient capacity may be invalid. In some cases, court-appointed guardianship/conservatorship may be required.

Build a specialist team (early):

- **Medical:** primary care + neurologist; consider a neuropsychological evaluation for formal capacity assessment and care planning.
- **Legal:** an **elder law** or **special needs** attorney for Powers of Attorney, advance directives, HIPAA releases, trusts, and (when necessary) guardianship.
- **Care coordination:** a **geriatric care manager** (Aging Life Care Professional) to evaluate safety, services, and care settings, along with a social worker for community resources.

Care choices will evolve.
Who you choose as the **caregiver**, and the **level of long-term care**

(in-home help, adult day programs, memory care, skilled nursing) will be influenced by safety risks (wandering, falls), behavioral symptoms, medication management, and the ability to perform Activities of Daily Living. Reassess regularly. Plan for **respite** to prevent caregiver burnout.

Use this book wisely.

- Lean on the **checklists and guides** to get organized and ask better questions.
- Then get **tailored guidance** from your medical team and an elder law attorney in your state. Laws and options vary by jurisdiction.

When to seek help now (not later):
Wandering or getting lost; unsafe driving; missed meds; aggression or rapid behavior change; signs of neglect or financial exploitation; repeated falls. Call emergency services for immediate safety concerns.

Trusted starting points:

- **Alzheimer's Association 24/7 Helpline: 800-272-3900** (support, education, local resources
- **Eldercare Locator (U.S. Administration for Community Living): 800-677-1116** (connects you to local aging services).
- **Find an elder law attorney (NAELA).**
- **Find a geriatric care manager (Aging Life Care Association).**
- **Caregiving guidance from NIA/Alzheimers.gov**

Three Key Questions

1. What level of care is needed?
2. Where will you receive that care?
3. How will we pay for it?

What level of care do I need?

We already discussed how care ebbs and flows, rather than being linear. This explains why caregiving comes on slowly before evolving into a full-time commitment.

Common Stages of Long-Term Care

Casual

- **In-Home Assistance:** Meal prep, cleaning, errands.
- **Independent Living Communities:** Safe environments with social opportunities.

Medical

1. **Part- or Full-Time Nursing Help:** For medication, mobility, or hygiene.

2. **Assisted Living Facilities:** Support with Activities of Daily Living (ADLs). We'll explain this in depth shortly.

3. **Memory Care:** For Alzheimer's or dementia-specific needs. We'll discuss some specifics soon as well.

4. **Continuing Care Retirement Communities (CCRCs):** Offering graduated care as needs change. The benefits of these places are that they are suitable even as you advance from casual to advanced needs, but they give the stability of one location.

Advanced

5. **Specialized Care Facilities:** For diseases like Parkinson's, MS, or stroke.
6. **Memory Care:** For Alzheimer's or dementia-specific needs.
7. **Hospice:** Focused on comfort in end-of-life situations.
8. **Respite Care:** Short-term care to relieve family caregivers.

Qualifying for Long-Term Care Benefits

To qualify for long-term care (LTC) insurance benefits, a person must typically be unable to perform at least **two of the six Activities of Daily Living (ADLs)**. The insurance company will require a signed statement from a physician to verify it. S**ignificant cognitive impairment** will also qualify you, which may be the result of a traumatic brain injury, stroke, coma, Alzheimer's, or Dementia. Being in a wheelchair alone doesn't qualify you. It must also be tied to the ADLs.

Remember BEDCOT.

1. Bathing
2. Eating
3. Dressing
4. Continence
5. Toileting (the ability to get on and off a toilet).
6. Transferring (bed to toilet, wheelchair to bathtub)

Where will I live?

The Stigma of "Facilities"

"I don't want to be put in some facility." This is often said with bitterness, perhaps accompanied by a sneer across your face. You may be thinking of a cold, clinical, and downright depressing place. People often recall the difficult stories from the COVID-19 pandemic. A facility means they have hospital-grade staff and equipment to address complex medical needs. Rather than staying in a hospital bed, you have a room that's your own. The quality and comfort of that room depend on choices made long before care is needed.

Ultimately, you need to find a place that is comfortable, safe, and accommodating to your specific needs, wants, and budget.

A Word of Caution

In the upcoming discussion on family dynamics, we will talk about the family abuser. Before we get into it, you must be aware that abuse doesn't only happen behind closed doors at home. It can also occur under the banner of "professional care." Hiring in-home aides, moving into assisted living, or trusting a facility doesn't guarantee safety.

- Some aides misuse access to finances, medications, or personal information.
- Some facilities cut corners on staffing or training, leaving residents neglected.
- Even licensed professionals can cross the line into exploitation or abuse if oversight is weak.

That's why **vetting and monitoring are critical**. This makes family involvement, advocacy, and vigilance just as crucial as choosing the right legal or financial plan. Background checks, references, surprise visits, and regular conversations with both the caregiver and the loved one all make a difference. And remember: a glossy brochure or a professional license is not the same as trust.

Choosing the Right Care

These are the two primary paths families navigate once care needs arise:

- **In-Home Care** — bringing help to you.
- **On-Site Care** — moving into a professional facility.

There shouldn't be any question about what the person needing care wants here. We already discussed the role of the family caregiver. If that's not the best option, here's how to think about the other two routes. The earlier you chart your course, the smoother the journey will be when care needs change.

In-Home Care: Support Where You Live

This tends to be the preferred option for most seniors. "The only way I'm leaving my home is in a body bag" may be how your husband shares his preferences. The desire to age in place, in the comfort of one's own home or in a loved one's home, is often preferred. Keep in mind that modifications to the home may be necessary, including grab bars and wheelchair ramps. Another consideration may be having laundry, a bathroom, a bedroom, and a kitchen all on one floor. You'll also want to look at general home safety and the home's condition.

Non-Medical Help

- Concierge services: groceries, errands, driving.
- House cleaning.
- Companionship and light assistance.

- Home Health Aide (HHA): Light meal prep, social interaction, errands, pet care, household tasks.
    - Cost: often $35–$70+/hour. Locally, this can amount to $300,000/year for 24/7 in-home support.

Medical Professionals

- **Certified Nursing Assistant (CNA):** Monitors vitals, provides medication support, mobility/lift assistance, and minor wound care.
- **Registered Nurse (RN):** Oversees higher-level medical care at home.

On-Site Communities: From Lifestyle to Full-Time Care

When the home is unsuitable or no longer ideal, on-site care becomes necessary.

Independent Retirement Communities (Non-Medical)

- Designed for healthy, active older adults.
- Provide housing, meals, housekeeping, transportation, and social activities.
- Residents live independently, but with a built-in community and conveniences.
- Medical care is not part of the package (though outside services can often be brought in).
- Example: "55+ retirement living" or "continuing care campus" in the independent living wing.

Assisted Living (Medical Support Begins)

- Combines housing, meals, and personal care support (bathing, dressing, toileting).
- Staff provide daily assistance but not hospital-level care.
- Offers social activities and some health monitoring.
- Costs vary but are generally less than memory care or skilled nursing.

Memory Care (Specialized Medical Community)

- Assisted living services + dementia/Alzheimer's-specific care.
- Secure environment to prevent wandering.
- Staff trained in cognitive conditions.
- Specialized activities: music therapy, reminiscence, pet therapy.
- Higher cost due to enhanced safety and training.

Skilled Nursing Facilities (SNFs)

- 24/7 medical oversight.
- Suitable for rehab, chronic illness, or full-time nursing care.
- Different from assisted living: more medical staff, less independence.

Factors to Consider Across Communities

- Medical vs. non-medical support needed.
- Lifestyle vs. healthcare emphasis.
- Amenities, activities, and sense of community.

- Cost and payment methods.
- Location and proximity to family.

Memory Care vs. Assisted Living

Category	Memory Care	Assisted Living
Core Services	Housing, meals, bathing assistance, and toileting support	Housing, meals, bathing assistance, toileting support
Specialized Features	Staff trained in dementia and Alzheimer's care; secure, monitored environment to prevent wandering	General caregiving staff; standard safety measures
Therapeutic Programming	Specialized activities such as music therapy, art therapy, reminiscence therapy, and pet therapy	Social activities like games, group outings, clubs, and holiday events
Cost	Higher cost due to specialized dementia care and enhanced safety measures	Generally lower cost compared to memory care

How do we pay for it?

The path you choose here doesn't just affect dollars; it determines whether you and your family have **options and control**, or whether you're stuck in a crisis with few choices and mounting stress.

Yes, care can be expensive. A full-time memory care home may cost $15,000 per month, while assisted living can average $7,700 per month. The real crisis isn't the price tag. It's arriving at that moment without a plan.

Without clarity, savings are drained in panic. Assets are spent down without a strategy. Family members argue over whether to sell the house. Care decisions get made by whoever shows up in the ER first. The legacy you spent a lifetime building doesn't just get depleted; it gets **scattered**, because no one knew your wishes. You may want your ashes scattered, but not your family.

With clarity, the same numbers tell a different story.

- You know whether insurance, personal assets, or Medicaid will be the first line of defense.
- You've decided what "legacy" means to you, whether it's leaving money, memories, or simply peace.
- Your family isn't stuck asking "what would Mom have wanted?" while writing checks they can't afford.

Funding Options

- **Personal Assets**
  Most flexible but quickly depleted. The average American nearing retirement has between $460,000 and $610,000 saved. Whether that lasts two decades or two years depends less on the amount and more on whether there's a plan.

  ☑ More choice in facilities, providers, and amenities.

  ☑ Faster access to care.

  ✕ Expensive and can quickly deplete savings without planning.

- **Stand-Alone Long-Term Care Insurance**
  Requires medical documentation and approval.

- **Life Insurance or an annuity with a care rider**
  A *rider* is an add-on to an insurance policy that provides extra benefits beyond the base coverage. A care rider allows a life insurance policy to also pay for long-term care expenses under certain conditions. Riders can be powerful, but it's essential to understand the fine print: eligibility rules, medical triggers, and legal specifications often determine whether you can actually use the benefits.
  - The definitions for chronic and terminal illness are defined in the contract language. Read this carefully and consult with a professional, preferably someone who isn't selling the policy. These typically carry fees, i.e., higher commissions for the agents selling them, so be cautious.
- **Medicaid**
  For those with limited means. Please note that eligibility is subject to asset and income restrictions, as well as a 5-year lookback period on transfers.

\+ Covers nursing homes and extended care for eligible individuals.

\+ Limited choice: not all facilities accept Medicaid.

\- Bureaucracy: delays and paperwork can be significant.

- **Medicare (Limited Coverage)**
  Remember from the Medicare chapter that Part A covers skilled nursing after a qualifying hospitalization, but not long-term custodial care.

Clarity Affirmations

- Now I know caregiving affects every part of life.
- I can talk with my family about roles and responsibilities.

- I understand that caregiving is a shared journey, not a solo task.
- I will prepare with compassion and clarity.

Action Plan

With the right tools, caregiving can be guided by love and understanding, rather than chaos. The earlier you set your course, the more likely it is to be a blessing rather than a burden.

1. **If you are a caregiver in crisis:**
   Create a written care plan. Track expenses. Seek respite and support.

2. **If your parents are showing signs that help may be needed:**
   Have "the talk." Review their legal documents. Tour care facilities early. Do this before the crisis arrives.

3. **If you're planning for yourself:**
   Estimate the future cost of care. Review long-term care coverage. Name your decision-makers before someone decides for you.

4. **Get professional guidance.**
   Elder law attorneys, care coordinators, and financial planners can save you years of stress and thousands of dollars.

Final Thoughts

Aging isn't something we can avoid, but how we prepare for it makes all the difference. Whether you're a caregiver or someone planning your future, the earlier you begin these conversations and legal preparations, the more options and peace you may have.

And remember: Caregiving is more than a responsibility. It's a sacred, difficult, and deeply meaningful act of love.

Looking Ahead

We'll discuss **hospice, grief, and the final chapter of care**, a topic often avoided, but one of the most sacred and necessary. We'll also explore how families can honor loved ones well and begin the process of healing and legacy transfer.

CHAPTER TWELVE

End of Life Planning: Compassion or Chaos?

"Grief is the price we pay for love."

Queen Elizabeth II

Eventually, every care journey reaches its closing chapter — a point on the map where the destination is clear, and the route ahead changes.

Hospice. Death. Grief.

The question isn't whether you'll face this. You will. The question is how: with rest or chaos.

Take me out behind the barn. That's what people say when I mention aging and end-of-life care. Some chuckle nervously. Some mean it. These aren't plans. They're desperate jokes and whispered fears, ways of saying, *"I don't want to suffer, and I don't want to be a burden."*

A plan is discussed, documented, and shared. Otherwise, these paths could be a nightmare for your family, another painful decision your family will be forced to make for you. If you don't decide, they will. The memory they'll carry isn't your peaceful exit; instead, it's the sound of one sibling screaming at another in the hallway: *"You killed Dad."*

If you've ever watched someone decline, you know the truth: death rarely comes clean, quick, or easy. It's messy and it's hard. Messy may look like decisions about machines and morphine, then gasping for air and last breaths. Then the body goes cold and blood drains from the face. Do I have your attention yet?

When families avoid talking about it, the end can become chaotic, traumatic, and filled with second-guessing that lingers for years. Aging and dying are inevitable. You can joke about it, or you can make a plan. But if you want your dignity preserved, your family protected, and your legacy intact, you cannot afford to leave this conversation undone.

Chaos or Clarity? The Choice Is Yours

Without a plan:

- Confusion over what mom would have wanted because no one ever asked, and nothing was written down.
- Guilt that medication ended life too soon, or prolonged it too long.
- A family divided by resentment instead of united in love.
- Final days filled with panic, paperwork, and second-guessing.

With a plan:

- Brothers sitting together in quiet remembrance, not arguing over paperwork.
- A letter in Dad's handwriting, read aloud through tears, which gives a blessing, not division.
- Trust in a care plan that was discussed and documented while he was still able to speak.
- A daughter free to hold her mother's hand, not a stack of unpaid bills.
- A family laughing through photo albums, not fighting over who has Power of Attorney.
- Memories made in the final days as stories are told, forgiveness is exchanged, and prayers are whispered.

Peace doesn't arrive by accident. It's prepared for.

Legacy isn't just what you leave behind in accounts and property. It's how your family honors your memory.

The Caregiver's Responsibility
Here's the hard truth: **you are responsible for the difference.**

End-of-life care on paper is about comfort, dignity, and support. In reality, it can feel rushed, clinical, even cold, unless someone speaks up. Doctors, nurses, and care teams mean well, but

No one knows your loved one's story, values, and wishes better than you.

You must be their voice. Advocacy isn't optional; it's the only way to make sure what was promised is what's delivered.

3 Different Paths, One Responsibility

There is no single way to approach the end of life. But there is one responsibility: to choose.

Option 1: Death With Dignity

Option 2: Hospice

Option 3: Natural Decline

There isn't one "right" path, but there is one common truth: **if you don't plan, the choice won't be yours.** It will be made for you.

The last days can either be filled with panic, guilt, and argument. On the other hand, it can be a time of presence, forgiveness, and peace. The difference doesn't come from the system. It comes from preparation and presence.

Option 1: Death with Dignity

Hard Questions, Harder Choices

Some people get to die on their own terms. Others… just wait.
A widowed man now in hospice care is slowly fading. His loving daughter and caregiver sits at his bedside. She's been caring for his every need, and now it's close to the end. He quietly asks, *Why is this taking so long? I'm ready to reunite with my wife.*

In moments like these, families wrestle with deeply emotional, spiritual, and complex questions. If you could end your own suffering on your own terms, would you?

For some, hospice isn't the only end-of-life decision. In several states, "Death with Dignity" laws allow a terminally ill, mentally competent adult to request and self-administer prescribed medication to end life peacefully. This is sometimes referred to as *Medical Aid in Dying (MAID).*

This option is controversial. For some families, it represents compassion: avoiding prolonged suffering, choosing to pass on their own terms, and sparing loved ones from watching a slow decline. For others, it conflicts with deeply held spiritual or ethical beliefs.

Where it's legal today (as of 2025): Oregon, Washington, California, Colorado, Hawaii, Maine, New Jersey, New Mexico, Vermont, Washington D.C., and Montana (through court ruling). Each state has its own criteria, but standard requirements include:

- The individual must be a resident of the state.
- Two physicians must certify that the patient has a terminal illness with six months or less to live.
- The patient must make multiple verbal and written requests.
- The patient must be able to self-administer the medication.

Arguments in favor: autonomy, relief from suffering, peace of mind.
Arguments against: moral or religious objections, fear of subtle family pressure, or slippery-slope concerns.

Why This Matters
Whether or not you would ever choose it, *Death with Dignity* is part of the modern landscape of end-of-life care. Clarity before crisis means discussing it openly, so families aren't blindsided if it comes up. Even deciding *against it* is a form of planning, because it protects loved ones from agonizing over what you "would have wanted."

Death with Dignity is not about choosing death; it's about choosing how to face it when it comes.

Option 2: Hospice

Textbook vs Reality

Hospice care is specialized care focused on comfort, dignity, and quality of life during the final stages of a terminal illness. It does **not** mean giving up. It means choosing a different path, one focused on peace, not a cure. Hospice care focuses on managing pain, reducing stress, and providing emotional, spiritual, and practical support to patients and their families.

Raw Truth: "Care" may feel like chaos

I've heard families whisper that hospice killed the patient. They describe painkillers that left their loved one incoherent or with a sudden decline after enrollment. Some say they felt pressured into signing papers. Others felt their parent was treated as though the end had already arrived. Whether medically accurate or not, perception is reality for the grieving, so those perceptions turn into scars if no plan exists. This is why advocacy matters, because if you don't lead, fear will.

- Will your family know when to say "enough," or will that choice be forced on them?
- Will you understand what medications will be given, and why, or will you be blindsided when your loved one slips away faster than expected?
- Will you choose your hospice provider, or will a hospital social worker choose for you?

Why Hospice Matters

Hospice doesn't mean giving up; it means choosing how the last chapter is written: with dignity, relief, and a sense of connection.

Benefits include:

- Relief from pain and difficult symptoms
- A calming, supportive environment
- More time spent at home (if desired)
- Guidance on legal, financial, and emotional matters
- Comfort for the patient and peace for the family

For many, hospice becomes a sacred time, an opportunity to say what needs to be said, to reflect, to forgive, and to simply be present.

Hospice vs. Palliative Care

These terms are often used interchangeably, but they're not the same.

- **Palliative care** can be given **at any stage** of illness and **alongside curative treatment**. It focuses on symptom relief and emotional support.

- **Hospice care** is for those who **stop curative treatments** and are nearing the end of life.

In many cases, a person begins with palliative care and transitions to hospice later. Medicare covers both under different guidelines.

When Hospice Makes Sense

Families often wait too long to consider hospice, entering at the height of a storm rather than setting their course when waters are still calm enough to navigate. Here are signs it may be time:

- Ongoing hospitalizations with no improvement
- Declining appetite, weight loss, or frailty
- Pain that's difficult to control
- Confusion, agitation, or withdrawal
- Caregiver burnout and emotional exhaustion

Hospice can take place:

- In your home
- At a hospice residence
- In a hospital or nursing home
- Through visiting hospice nurses and teams

To qualify for hospice under Medicare:

- Two doctors must certify that the patient has **six months or less** to live (if the illness runs its usual course)
- The patient must choose to **forgo curative treatment**
- The goal becomes **comfort over cure**

This can be a hard decision, but for many families, it brings incredible relief and freedom.

Common Conditions Covered by Hospice

Hospice is typically available to those with a life expectancy of six months or less due to terminal illness. These may include:

- Cancer
- Advanced AIDS
- End-stage diabetes
- Stroke (with severe complications)
- End-stage renal disease
- Dementia and Alzheimer's
- Parkinson's disease
- Huntington's disease
- Multiple sclerosis
- Congestive heart failure
- Heart valve disorders

These conditions often involve a progressive decline in function, and hospice steps in when curative treatment is no longer effective or desired.

Understanding Medicare Hospice Benefits

Understanding hospice benefits now is like studying the map before you set out. When the moment arrives, you'll know exactly which resources are available and how to access them without delay.

Hospice care is fully covered under **Medicare Part A**, provided specific criteria are met:

- The individual has been diagnosed with a terminal illness and has a life expectancy of six months or less.
- The patient elects **palliative care** (comfort-focused), rather than continuing treatments intended to cure the illness.
- A written agreement is signed to begin hospice care, although patients may withdraw and pursue curative treatment again if desired.

What Medicare Covers

Covered does but not necessarily free, so deductibles and co-pays may apply.

Medical Care & Support

- Visits from doctors and nurses
- Nursing care (including skilled nursing under certain conditions)
- Prescription medications for pain relief and symptom management
- Medical equipment (e.g., hospital bed, wheelchair, oxygen)
- Medical supplies (e.g., bandages, catheters, gloves)

Personal Care

- Home health aide services
- Hospice aide and homemaker services
- Physical, occupational, and speech therapy (as needed for comfort)

Counseling & Family Support

- Emotional and spiritual counseling (for both patient and family)
- Social worker services
- Dietary and nutritional counseling
- Bereavement support for family (up to 13 months after death)

Inpatient & Respite Services

- Short-term inpatient care for pain or symptom management
- Short-term respite care (up to 5 days for caregiver relief)

Out-of-pocket costs are minimal for most families. Hospice teams also help coordinate services, manage symptoms, and support the emotional and spiritual needs of both patients and their caregivers.

Choosing a Hospice Provider

Don't be afraid to ask questions. This is about choosing the right guide for the last stretch of the journey.

Not all hospice agencies are the same. When choosing a provider, consider:

- **Experience and reputation**: How long have they served your community?
- **Range of services**: Do they offer 24/7 support, bereavement counseling, and spiritual care?
- **Team communication**: Are they transparent, collaborative, and responsive?
- **Insurance compatibility**: Are they Medicare-certified? Do they accept your plan?
- **Continuity of care**: Will they support your transition from home to inpatient if needed?

Don't be afraid to ask questions. You are interviewing them as much as they are assessing the situation. Choose the team that best matches your family's values and needs.

The Hospice Team

A hospice team provides holistic, interdisciplinary support to the patient and family. That team may include:

- **Physicians**: Guide the overall plan of care
- **Nurses**: Manage medications, symptoms, and medical needs
- **Hospice aides**: Help with bathing, grooming, dressing
- **Social workers**: Assist with emotional, logistical, and legal support
- **Counselors and chaplains**: Provide emotional and spiritual comfort
- **Volunteers**: Offer companionship, support, and light errands
- **Therapists**: Physical, occupational, and speech therapists may assist as needed

Together, they form a compassionate safety net, ensuring no one faces the end alone.

Option 3: Natural Decline

1. **VSED (Voluntarily Stopping Eating and Drinking)**
   A deliberate decision to stop taking food and fluids, usually supported by palliative care to manage discomfort such as dry mouth, anxiety, or agitation. Families should be aware that this process often lasts days to weeks, not hours.
2. **Allowing Natural Progression of Illness**
   Choosing to stop aggressive medical interventions (hospitalizations, transfusions, dialysis, chemotherapy, surgeries) and allowing the underlying illness to take its natural course. Often combined with comfort-focused care at home.

3. **DNR / DNI (Do Not Resuscitate / Do Not Intubate)**
These orders prevent mechanical ventilation, CPR, or intubation. It doesn't mean "no care," but instead avoiding invasive measures that can prolong suffering when quality of life is already low.

4. **Stopping or Withdrawing Treatments**
Families may decide to discontinue treatments like dialysis, ventilators, or feeding tubes when they no longer align with the patient's wishes or quality of life goals. This is legally and ethically distinct from euthanasia — it's allowing the illness to progress without further intervention.

5. **Faith-Based Surrender / "Letting God Decide"**
For many, the natural decline is framed as an act of faith. This can include continuing ordinary care (food, fluids as tolerated, comfort measures), but not choosing interventions to extend life artificially. The emphasis is on spiritual readiness, prayer, and community support.

Supporting the Dying, and the Living

End-of-life care is about more than the person dying; it's about guiding everyone involved toward closure, understanding, and healing. This gives direction when emotions and grief can easily pull people off course. As death approaches:

- Keep communication open
- Allow for meaningful conversations, prayers, and closure
- Respect spiritual or cultural rituals
- Invite hospice chaplains, counselors, or clergy if helpful

After death:

- Expect waves of emotion
- Let grief take its course, there is no "normal" timeline
- Avoid major financial or legal decisions in the first weeks if possible
- Use what's learned in estate planning to guide next steps: Will or Trust execution, beneficiary claims, property transitions

We'll cover more of the grief and estate transfer process later, but for now, focus on presence over paperwork.

If you've followed the estate planning steps, these processes should go more smoothly.

Letters, Videos, and Final Words

These are like waypoints you leave for those following behind, markers of your values, love, and life story that help guide your family long after you're gone.

One of the most beautiful acts of planning is **leaving something personal behind**, a legacy of love, not just assets.

Consider:

- Writing letters to your children or grandchildren
- Recording a video message
- Creating a family blessing or faith testimony
- Donating to a cause in your name
- Sharing stories that shaped your life

These don't require money. They require heart.

The Role of the Faith Community

No matter which path you choose, churches, spiritual advisors, and faith communities often play a critical role in end-of-life care. They offer:

- Support for caregivers
- Guidance for funeral or memorial services
- Counseling and grief recovery groups
- Help organize meals, visits, and logistics

If you or your family are part of a faith tradition, don't be afraid to lean on your community.

Clarity Affirmations

- Now I know end-of-life planning is an act of love.
- I can bring peace to my family through preparation.
- I understand that avoiding the conversation creates confusion.
- I will face the future with courage and compassion.

Action Plan

1. **Map out your end-of-life plan in advance.** Know your coverage, preferences, and providers before deciding what's urgent. Learn about the benefits your Medicare or insurance plan offers. Most include medications, equipment, and home visits.

2. **Discuss end-of-life wishes early.** Don't wait until someone is too sick to speak. Use your Living Will, Physician Orders for Life-Sustaining Treatment (POLST), or advance directive as a guide.

3. **Plan your final message.** Write, record, or share your thoughts while you still can.
4. **Support the grieving.** If you're not the one grieving, be the one who listens, remembers, and shows up.
5. **Talk with your doctor.** Ask if hospice is appropriate based on current health conditions and prognosis.
6. **Schedule a hospice consultation.** Most hospice agencies will provide an assessment at no charge.
7. **Review your Medicare or insurance coverage**. Ensure hospice benefits are in place and understood.
8. **Involve your family.** Have open discussions about end-of-life goals, preferences, and concerns.
9. **Select your provider carefully.** Use the criteria above to choose a team that aligns with your values.
10. **Update legal documents**. Ensure your Power of Attorney, Will, and advance directives reflect current wishes.
11. **Create a care plan**. Decide if hospice will begin at home, in a specialty care environment, or transition as needed.
12. **Seek emotional and spiritual support.** Don't wait until things are difficult; grief support and counseling are available before and after passing.
13. **Plan for aftercare**. Funeral preferences, asset distribution, and family communication are easier when prepared in advance.
14. **Permit yourself to rest**. Hospice is also for the caregiver. Accept the help. Use respite care. You are not alone.

Final Thoughts

No one is ever fully ready to say goodbye. But the way you prepare determines whether that goodbye is marked by chaos or by peace. End-of-life care can take many forms: hospice, Death with Dignity where it's legal, natural decline, or faith-led acceptance. None of these paths is easy, but each can be meaningful when chosen with clarity.

Peace doesn't arrive by accident. It comes from preparation, presence, and advocacy. It comes from writing down your wishes, sharing them with your family, and insisting that the care promised is the care delivered.

In the end, your legacy is not only the money or property you leave behind; it's the memory of how you left. Will your family remember panic, arguments, and unanswered questions? Or will they remember your love, your presence, and the gift of peace you've given them by ensuring your wishes were communicated?

The choice is yours. Not whether death will come, but how it will be faced, and how your family will carry it forward.

Looking Ahead

You've held on this long, so now it's time for the climax as we'll turn to **relationship dynamics**: how families can strengthen or shatter under the weight of money, legacy, and unmet expectations.

Hospice brings the end into view, but family conflict often starts long before and continues long after.

Let's talk about how to protect your relationships as much as your wealth.

CHAPTER THIRTEEN

Relationship Dynamics: Human Side of Aging

"Family is not an important thing. It is everything."

Michael J. Fox

Even the most perfect financial and legal plan can unravel if the family holding it together falls apart. Aging isn't just technical, it's relational. Beneath every trust, power of attorney, or care plan is an undercurrent of history, expectations, and emotions. If those currents aren't acknowledged, they will steer the family into conflict when clarity is needed most.

This chapter isn't about numbers or protecting tangible property. It's about the people left to live with those numbers and whether they are fractured or united when it matters most. It's about preserving peace. It's about building a plan that honors your loved ones in life *and* in legacy.

Part I: Common Tensions and Family Dynamics

Case Study: The Cottage Revisited

Earlier, I shared the story of my grandmother's cottage, a place full of life, laughter, and love. It was where we gathered as a big family, celebrated traditions, and made countless memories. But over time, tension simmered beneath the surface. There were differences in involvement, in expectations, and in opinions, many of which were never fully addressed.

When my grandmother passed, the cottage became more than a property. It became a symbol of everything left unsaid and unresolved. There was no clear plan for its use, care, or ownership. Family members couldn't agree on how to handle her care, her finances, or the future of the cottage. Without a unified plan, the emotional weight of the moment took over.

And just like that, Grandma was gone. So was the cottage. So were the holidays as we knew them. It didn't have to end that way.

When I think about one of the most caring, generous people I've ever known, I can't help but remember how fractured things became in the end. That's not her legacy, but it's what we were left to navigate.

The truth: this wasn't a greedy family. It was a grieving one. But grief was made heavier by a lack of clarity, years of unequal roles, and unspoken assumptions that came to the surface too late.

Why Families Break Down (Even with a Plan)

A flawless estate plan and a fully funded care strategy can still collapse without communication. Old wounds resurface, assumptions fester, and unspoken expectations divide. The most significant threats to aging well are often emotional, not financial.

You've seen it, maybe even in your own family: disagreements about "what Mom would have wanted," resentment over who did the caregiving, or fights about money that are really fights about love and recognition.

The Power of a Conversation

"The most important planning tool isn't a Trust. It's a conversation."

I recently met Barry, a father of two wonderful daughters and grandfather to four grandchildren. His story is a perfect example of the importance of life planning. When I asked about his estate and care goals, he knew **exactly** what he wanted. He had a well-written trust and two smart daughters, so what could go wrong?

A lot, even though he knew what he wanted. He had plans to age in place, hire a private nurse, and had space in his home for private care.

His annuities had chronic and terminal illness provisions to pay for it. He had checked out a couple of local care facilities in case he needed to move. He planned to sell the house to pay for care if the annuities weren't enough. His trust laid out everything for his assets. His Power of Attorney documents were well-defined. It's rare to meet someone in my line of work who has put this much thought and planning into their aging.

But none of his wishes for his care were in writing. And worse, he hadn't discussed any of it with his daughters. They had **legal authority, but no clarity**. Conflict was inevitable.

Trust can distribute assets. But only a conversation can preserve peace.

Ask yourself:

- Have I clearly explained my wishes?
- Have I involved the right people in planning?
- Have I listened to how my family feels?
- Have I prepared others for the roles I've given them?

These conversations can be difficult. But they often spark healing and shape the true legacy we leave behind.

And when the journey reaches its last chapter, when decisions about care, decline, or even death itself must be made, these conversations are what keep families from falling into chaos.

Understanding Family Types

Every family is unique, but many follow predictable patterns. Recognizing yours helps you plan with compassion.

Family Type	Description	Planning Tip
Invincibles	"I'm not dying."	Frame planning as a gift, not something to fear.
Controllers	"I have it all handled."	Invite family input to reduce future conflict.
All Business	Focused on logistics	Balance spreadsheets with emotion.
Blended Families	Stepchildren, remarriage	Be explicit in documents. Fair doesn't always mean equal.
Equalizers	"Everyone gets the same."	Consider needs and history, not just numbers.

The Flavor of Dysfunction

When one family member becomes vulnerable, old dynamics often resurface, and new ones emerge.

It's time to become vulnerable, open, and honest about yourself and your family. Every family has its own unique flavor of dysfunction. Some of the stories you hear about are like a crazy episode of *Dr. Phil*, chair-throwing and all.

Take a moment and think about your family. Maybe there's an outcast who always stirs the pot. Another sibling is terrible with money. Someone else is never around. One wants everyone to get along. Maybe one child got everything from Mom and Dad, while you had to work for it all.

And if you're an only child? Then you carry the full weight yourself. You may hear the quiet (or not so quiet) refrain: *"You owe it to them after all they've given you."* That expectation can feel crushing when you're trying to juggle your own family, career, and well-being.

There may be another elephant in the room that we don't like to talk about: maybe the person you're now caring for or dealing with wasn't a saint. Some people weren't good parents. Perhaps they were absent, controlling, or even a jerk. Maybe you've never had a healthy adult relationship with them. Now you're being asked to step up in ways that stir up decades of unresolved hurt.

A mom who belittled her kids for decades now needs them to bathe and feed her, so now they're torn between duty and resentment.

I once worked with a woman caring for her mother. She described a mean and hurtful parent, someone who had never given her the love she craved. Caring for her mom was taking a heavy toll, so I finally asked why she kept trying so hard. Her eyes filled as she whispered: *"Because maybe she'll finally tell me she loves me."*

The Picture-Perfect Myth

On the outside, families often look picture-perfect, like that holiday photo where everyone is smiling in matching sweaters. In the world of social media, people have gotten good at presenting what they want others to see. But behind the frames and filters, the ugly parts come rushing back: grudges, favoritism, financial stress, and years of tension simmering just below the surface.

You might be thinking, *"But my kids get along. I love my siblings."* That may be true until there's money involved. A Will, a house, or an inheritance can suddenly become a chance to prove to Mom and Dad that you were the best, the most deserving, or the one who sacrificed the most. That's when the fractures often reveal themselves. That picture can get especially tattered around…

Politics, Religion, and Lifestyle

Lately, I've noticed another growing divide: politics, religion, and lifestyle. Families cut ties, siblings unfriend each other, and deep rifts form over values and beliefs. Those fractures don't magically disappear when care or inheritance enters the picture; they often get magnified.

Are you going to disinherit your daughter because she married someone of a different faith? Are you ready to cut your son out of the Will because he votes differently from you? Would you rather avoid your dying parent than sit through one more lecture about your life choices?

These are the conversations I hear behind closed doors:

- A brother who refuses to enter his sister's home because of her politics.
- A daughter who hasn't spoken to her dad in years, now faced with making his medical decisions.
- A mother rewriting her estate plan to "send a message" to the child whose lifestyle she can't accept.

This is the reality: the values that divide us at the dinner table don't suddenly disappear at the hospital bed. They show up stronger. And unless you name them, face them, and plan around them, they will tear families apart at the exact moment when unity matters most.

Other Sources of Conflict

Blended families add another layer of complexity. Stepsiblings may have vastly different loyalties. A second spouse may feel like an outsider to the "first family." Children from different marriages may question whether the estate will be "split fairly." Sometimes the tensions aren't even spoken aloud, but they hang in the air, shaping every conversation.

Distance can be another factor. One child lives nearby and withstands most of the caregiving, while another, states or even countries away, drops in with strong opinions but little follow-through. Resentment builds quickly when one sibling feels like the hands-on caregiver while others remain armchair critics.

Then there's the issue of in-laws. A daughter-in-law or son-in-law may push for decisions that serve their spouse's interests, stirring suspicion and conflict. In some families, the loudest voices at the table aren't even the children, but the partners they marry.

When you consider all these factors, such as sibling roles, old wounds, politics, religion, blended families, distance, in-laws, money, and strained parent-child relationships, you begin to understand why family meetings often spiral out of control.

Grief and Denial

Another layer of family conflict often comes from the simple fact that people are grieving. And grief doesn't just show up after a funeral. It usually begins long before, as families watch a loved one decline or lose independence.

Psychologists have long described the **stages of grief**:

1. **Denial** – *"Dad is fine. You're overreacting."* Denial shields us from pain by pretending things aren't changing.
2. **Anger** – *"Why is this happening to us?"* Frustration often gets directed at doctors, siblings, or whoever is closest.
3. **Bargaining** – *"If we just try this treatment, maybe things will go back to normal."* It's the desperate search for control when life feels out of control.
4. **Depression** – *"This is too hard. I can't do this anymore."* Sadness and withdrawal are familiar when the weight of reality sets in.

5. **Acceptance** – *"This is happening. How do we face it together?"* Acceptance doesn't mean we like the situation, but we stop resisting it.

The stages don't come in order, and family members don't move through them at the same pace. One sibling may still be in denial while another is deep in anger or despair. That mismatch alone creates friction.

For some, getting too involved in care planning or decision-making feels like admitting their parent or spouse is fading (denial). So, they stay at a distance. And here's where it gets complicated: denial doesn't always look like silence or withdrawal. Sometimes it's the opposite: the sibling who avoids showing up daily may also be the loudest critic. They second-guess the caregiver's decisions, go around the caregiver to talk directly to doctors or attorneys, or stir up conflict at family meetings. To the caregiver, this feels like betrayal: *"You're not here when I need help, but you're quick to criticize the choices I'm making."* This is the paradox of denial. On the surface, it appears to be a matter of distance. Underneath, it often stirs up interference, conflict, and additional stress for both the caregiver and the loved one receiving care.

Understanding grief doesn't excuse unruly behavior, but it explains a lot of it. Recognizing that your brother's outbursts may be rooted in anger, or that your sister's silence may be depression, helps reframe the conflict. It shifts the question from *"Why are they being so difficult?"* to *"What are they grieving right now?"*

While denial is the most common face of anticipatory grief, families also fall back on other coping styles, such as avoidance, control, or martyrdom. Whatever the response, the result is often the same: conflict, silence, or resentment.

Most conflicts are grief and history colliding, but sometimes it moves into fraud, neglect, or outright abuse.

Enablers, Tension, and the Responsibility of Giving

Families are often shaped not just by financial planning but by the patterns of giving within them. Some parents continue to support adult children long after they should be financially independent. In many cases, this giving comes at the parents' own expense, draining their retirement savings, delaying their goals, and creating resentment rather than joy.

This raises important questions:

- Are you giving out of pity or out of love?
- Are you fostering independence, or quietly enabling dependency?
- Will those you support now step in to care for you later, or will the cycle continue?
- Are you teaching financial responsibility, or postponing the hard lessons?

Watching someone give to others to their own demise and destruction is hard to watch.

Some people would rather run out of money than face conflict.

Healthy giving is intentional. It sets boundaries and communicates values. It says, "I love you enough to help you, but also enough to let you grow." Unhealthy giving, by contrast, often blurs those lines and creates tension among siblings who watch the imbalance unfold.

I once worked with a father who gifted his son a million-dollar *vacation home*. Yeah, that one took me back for a minute. On paper, it looked generous. For the father, the gift was not only financial; it was emotional. It seemed like an attempt to buy love, or perhaps to make up for years of distance and regret. The problem is that money cannot mend what was never repaired. Instead, it widened the gap.

Another client inherited an IRA and spent more than $100,000 in a single weekend at dance clubs. The money was gone before the paperwork had even settled. That inheritance could have been a foundation for long-term security; instead, it became a fleeting memory of excess. Can you imagine saving and sacrificing for decades to have the money vanish so quickly? This one is a lesson in the use of Trusts to control distributions and prevent squandered spending, but also about how some people may choose to grieve.

On the other side of the spectrum are parents who give generously in financial terms but rarely give of themselves. They may provide comfort, but not time. They may fund opportunities, but fail to teach wisdom, discipline, or character. The result can be tragic: wealth passed down without guiding values, often squandered within a single generation.

Legacy is more than money. It is also the stewardship of relationships, the transfer of wisdom, and the character we help shape. True giving balances provision with guidance, generosity with responsibility, and love with accountability.

Part II: How to Navigate Forward

This chapter goes deeper than what most people expect from a financial planner. And that's intentional. Because even the best estate plan can unravel if the family holding it together falls apart. Money without peace rarely preserves a legacy.

That's why this isn't just "financial planning." It's life planning. It's about preparing for the human side of aging, such as grief, conflict, reconciliation, and hope. These are hard, emotional spaces, and no one should have to navigate them alone.

That's where a team comes in. Not just attorneys and financial advisors, but counselors, therapists, clergy, coaches, and mediators. Each has a role to play in helping families face old wounds, find common ground, and move toward healing. When the right voices are at the table, the family has a significantly better chance of navigating both the technical challenges and the relational storms.

The Ripple Effect of Silence

If you don't plan for your own care and estate, your children will be left to guess. Guessing creates guilt. Guilt creates division. And division becomes the legacy no parent wants.

Remember, aging isn't just about managing physical decline; it's about managing **relational shifts**, **emotional legacies**, and **family transitions**.

Family Meetings: Don't Wait for the Funeral

The most effective planning happens while everyone is alive and healthy.

What to Cover:

- Where documents are stored
- Who holds legal authority

- Caregiving expectations
- Funeral preferences
- Legacy or charitable intentions

You don't need to disclose dollar amounts, but you should offer a roadmap.

The Family Wealth Briefing: A Necessary Conversation

One of the most powerful tools I've seen is what I call a **Family Wealth Briefing**. It's where logistics, legacy, and love intersect. You can download a copy from my website.

This meeting doesn't focus on numbers; it focuses on clarity:

- Who has authority?
- What care is desired?
- What faith or funeral preferences exist?
- Where are the documents?
- Who carries which responsibilities?

It's not about the assets. It's about alignment.

Unequal Inheritance: Fair Isn't Always Equal

Parents sometimes leave more to one child than another. Reasons vary:

- One child is disabled or financially struggling
- Another child received more support earlier in life
- A family farm or business is being left to one heir
- A caregiver child made major personal sacrifices

These decisions can be valid. But they can also trigger deep resentment if they come as a surprise.

If you're considering unequal distribution:

- Put it in writing
- Discuss it while you're alive
- Express gratitude and context
- Avoid shaming or comparing your children

Transparency doesn't guarantee agreement. But secrecy guarantees confusion.

Faith, Forgiveness, and Protecting the Family Legacy

Families are messy, and some wounds run deep. On our own, it can feel impossible to look past the wrongs, especially if they've piled up for years. But I've seen that reconciliation becomes possible when we draw on something greater than ourselves.

For the Christian, that means remembering what has already taken place: acknowledging our sin, our need for a Savior, receiving grace, repenting, and asking for forgiveness. If we've been forgiven much, then we're called to extend that same grace. It doesn't make the hurt disappear, but it does make healing possible.

With the guidance of the Holy Spirit, what feels humanly impossible: forgiving an absent parent, releasing resentment toward a sibling, breaking free from bitterness, can actually happen. That's where reconciliation begins, and where generational cycles can finally be broken.

Other faith traditions hold to similar principles. In Buddhism and Hinduism, the concept of karma reminds us that holding onto bitterness perpetuates cycles of pain, while letting go can free us, and those who come after us, from repeating them. In Judaism, *teshuvah* is the act of returning and making amends, restoring right relationship. In Islam, forgiveness is both a divine attribute and a personal practice that brings peace to the heart. Across traditions, the path may be different, but the destination remains the same: reconciliation, freedom from resentment, and the opportunity to start anew.

But even if faith isn't part of your framework, the principle is the same: holding on to anger only multiplies the pain. Letting go creates space for peace in your heart, in your relationships, and in the legacy you leave behind.

We'll explore how to hold these conversations *after* a death, but don't wait until then. Start now.

Clarity Affirmations

- Now I know money is never just about math; it's about people.
- I can see how family dynamics affect every decision.
- I understand that communication prevents conflict.
- I will begin conversations that strengthen trust.

Action Plan

Here are some steps to help manage the emotional and relational complexities that come with aging and caregiving:

1. **Host a Family Meeting**
   • Discuss wishes, roles, responsibilities, and expectations.
   • Invite advisors (legal, financial, spiritual) to support clarity and neutrality.

2. **Update Your Documents**
   • Medical and General POA
   • Will and/or Trust
   • Beneficiary designations

3. **Write a Letter of Instruction**
   • Clarify funeral wishes, passwords, and personalized messages.
   • Specify how caregivers or family should be reimbursed or supported.
4. **Acknowledge and Embrace Your Family Type**
   • Name your dynamic. Is it "invincible", "all business", or "blended"?
   • Plan accordingly, identifying where flexibility, clarity, or empathy are most needed.
5. **Care for the Caregiver**
   • If that's you: take breaks, ask for help, and set boundaries.
   • If it's someone else: offer emotional and financial support, and recognize their effort.
6. **Plan for Your Own Legacy**
   • Do not leave the next generation guessing.
   • Your children will face the same questions. Give them answers, not problems.

Final Thoughts

At the heart of every plan is not a set of documents but a family. Clarity before crisis in relationships matters just as much as it does in finances or healthcare. Money can be rebuilt. Trust and peace are harder to restore once lost.

Legacy is never only about wealth. It is about the memories preserved, the wisdom passed down, and the ability of a family to sit together in peace rather than apart in silence. The choices you make now determine which of those legacies you leave behind.

CHAPTER FOURTEEN
After Death Part I: Grief

"What we have once enjoyed we can never lose. All that we love deeply becomes a part of us."

Helen Keller

Loss changes the room. Some moments feel hollow, others strangely normal. Grief doesn't march in order; it comes in waves of love, anger, relief, regret, sometimes in the same hour. This chapter is about making space for all of it.

You don't have to "be strong" or rush decisions. We'll name what grief can look like, why family members grieve differently, and how to care for yourself while caring for others. You'll get simple language for hard conversations, ideas for honoring a life, and signs it's time to call a counselor, pastor, or support group.

The goal here isn't to fix grief. It's to carry it with steadiness and compassion together.

In this chapter, you'll learn:

- What normal grief can feel like (and why there's no single timeline)
- How to support a spouse, children, and yourself
- How to set gentle boundaries in the first weeks
- Simple ways to remember well and begin to heal

CHAPTER FOURTEEN
After Death Part I: Grief

Dear Friend,

I want you to know something: many people come to an advisor like me for the very first time after a death. You may even feel like meeting with me, or any advisor, is just another errand, another box to check on a long to-do list. One more appointment after the doctor, the funeral home, and the attorney. We begin as strangers. You sit down across the table, weary from grief, carrying folders of papers you don't understand, pulled in a dozen directions, wondering what to do next.

- The attorney says, "You need to roll this over now."
- The bank asks, "How do you want to handle these accounts?"
- Family members wonder, "What's next?"

As I listen, an alarm often goes off inside me.

How can I give clear guidance when someone feels so lost? What should I prioritize first? How do I reassure without overwhelming?

So, I'm telling you the same way I tell them: you don't have to make every decision today. You don't have to know the answers right now. It's enough to simply be here. To breathe.

When you've just lost someone, it can feel like the sky is falling. Every envelope, every phone call, every form can look like an urgent priority. Your mind races: What if I miss something? What if I get it wrong?

But here's the truth: you've already walked through life and death. Compared to that, these tasks are not life-or-death. They are essential, but not all of them must be done today. They don't all have to be carried by you alone.

That's why I pause here, to remind you: even though everything feels urgent, you have permission to slow down.

My role is to help you distinguish between what needs attention now and what can wait, replacing panic with a plan.

In time, the path will come into focus. For now, the next step isn't a form or a signature; it's giving yourself the grace to pause.

One of the first things I often ask is: "Have you had time to grieve?" Almost always, the answer is, "No."

In these moments, I realize that person's vulnerability. They've trusted me with the weight of their story, often in its rawest form.

I'm not here to replace a grief counselor or to take you deeper into the emotions you're already carrying. I know your time and energy are precious right now. My role is different.

I listen because hearing your story, the crisis, the weight of what you've been through, is what equips me to give you clarity. I want to understand where you're coming from, what feels urgent, and what needs to be done next. That way, we can quiet the noise and focus on the few things that matter most at the moment.

So, I ask gentle questions, not because I need every detail, but because they honor your story: How long were you married? How did they pass? How long did this go on? How recent is the loss?

I often hear every detail, anyway, spoken through tears or silence. That's the moment when something shifts. The conversation isn't just about numbers. It's about tears, silence, and the weight of choices you never wanted to face. As I hear the story, I become invested in it.

In that shift, an advisor becomes something more: a confidant, a listener, a guide who helps steady the ground beneath your feet.

CHAPTER FOURTEEN
After Death Part I: Grief

I know something of this because I've lived it, too. I remember the moment I heard the news of my father's passing.

First came the shock and denial: wasn't he supposed to be coming home from the hospital again? Then the questions tumbled over me all at once: What now? Will we move? Will I have to change schools? What about my mom and sisters?

It felt like the ground gave way beneath me. Everything was uncertain, everything was heavy.

So, when I sit across from someone who has just lost a spouse, a parent, or a friend, I don't see a stack of papers or accounts. I see that younger version of myself, overwhelmed and asking questions I couldn't possibly answer. And I remember: what they need first is someone to listen, not tell them what to do.

Grief is not neat. It doesn't respect calendars or checklists. It comes in waves. Sometimes it looks like shock. Other times, like anger or bargaining. It can settle into depression before lifting toward acceptance, reconstruction, even hope. Some days you may feel strong. Other days, you may feel like you've gone backward. That's normal.

Grief doesn't always manifest as tears; sometimes it appears as conflict. I've often said: "They weren't greedy, they were grieving." A sibling may fight over a piece of furniture not because they want it, but because they're clinging to the person who sat in that chair. A child may lash out at the executor, not because of the money, but because anger feels safer than sorrow.

If you see conflict in the days ahead, remember grief wears many masks. It's rarely about the money itself. It's about pain.

For many caregivers, there is a second grief: the sudden absence of activity. No more doctors' appointments. No more schedules to juggle. No more medications to track. No more machines humming through the night.

And then, the room. Empty.

The very space that once felt crowded with responsibility now feels hollow. Some describe it as falling into a void, the stillness after years of constant motion. It can be as painful as the loss itself because it reminds you of just how much has changed.

If that's you, know this feeling is normal. It doesn't mean you are weak. It means you loved deeply. That silence reflects your devotion. In time, it may be filled again with rest, with memories, with new rhythms. For now, it's okay to sit in the quiet.

If that's where you find yourself, I want to pause and say: I'm sorry. I'm sorry for your loss, and for the weight you're carrying. You don't have to do everything perfectly. You don't have to figure it all out today.

If I can help at all, let it be this: let this chapter, along with the worksheet I have online, serve as a guide. Not to rush you. Not to overwhelm you, but to give you something to hold onto when it feels like everything else has been taken away.

The Empowered Widow

I haven't told you about Gabby yet, have I? Her husband of 50+ years had always been "the provider," the one who managed the finances. He used to say, *"As long as she has money to buy the groceries, she'll be alright."* Gabby's husband expressed his love through provision and protection. It sounds like he had good intentions, but when he died, she was not all right.

In her grief, she was suddenly handed legal documents she didn't understand, with account statements and bills she had never touched. She told me it had been years since she'd even balanced a checkbook.

Every envelope she opened, every form she faced, felt like a reminder that she was on her own now.

When she called my office to consolidate her accounts, I asked her gently how she was holding up. Her voice was quiet: *"It's been hard."* As I began asking about her plans for the money, she admitted, *"He always managed everything. I don't know what any of this stuff is. I've never had to deal with it. It was his way of protecting and providing for me. Now I'm completely lost and don't even know where to begin."*

Those words still stay with me. Yet what stands out most is what happened next. Gabby was sharp, eager to learn, and quick to grasp concepts once they were explained. We started small, focusing on the basics, and gradually expanded her understanding. Within a few calls, she began to find her footing. She discovered she was more capable than she realized.

Gabby's strength and determination allowed her to move through the stages of grief into acceptance. That didn't erase her grief, but it gave her hope. By the end, Gabby felt empowered, independent, and confident. When I asked how she wanted to use the money, her voice lifted: *"I want to travel. I haven't done that in years."* She even began planning a trip to spend time with her grandkids. She found a way to breathe again.

I was reminded of the strength my own mother showed when my father passed away. Personally, I cannot imagine the weight of losing a spouse. Walking through that loss personally gave me a deep compassion for others facing it.

Gabby's story reflects a reality faced by many families. In some marriages, both spouses take an active role, tracking investments and setting goals together. That level of shared involvement, however, is the exception. More often, one person takes the lead while the other remains in the background. It's understandable to be more passive and lead in different areas of the family. However, be cautious about avoiding engagement in financial discussions. When loss happens, the transition is likely to be even more overwhelming.

I concluded Gabby's husband had good intentions. Not every marriage does. For some, what begins as provision crosses into unhealthy control, even abuse.

Provider or Abuser?

The phrase, *"As long as she has enough to get groceries,"* still makes me cringe. Reducing a spouse's financial future to little more than survival is not love; it is neglect. Proper provision is about empowerment. It means ensuring that a spouse understands the essentials, knows which documents matter, and has relationships with trusted advisors who can step in when needed.

There is also a crucial distinction between a passive spouse or a strong provider mindset and outright abuse. Spousal abuse can take many forms: physical, emotional, or financial. Emotional abuse erodes identity and confidence. Physical abuse destroys trust and safety. When emotional abuse is present, victims may even excuse physical abuse or blame themselves for it. Financial abuse can create control so profoundly that a person feels powerless to leave.

Common Signs of Financial Abuse

- Being denied access to joint bank accounts, credit cards, or financial records.
- Not being allowed to work or being forced to hand over income.
- Having purchases, spending, or even basic needs tightly controlled.
- Being kept "in the dark" about bills, debts, or investments.
- Having property or accounts signed over under pressure or without a clear explanation.

- Facing threats of financial ruin, abandonment, or retaliation if independence is sought.

I have met people in these circumstances, and they often describe feeling trapped, as if living in a prison. Some remain because they "do not believe in divorce." Others divorce the abusive spouse only to face another heartbreak when their children turn against them for "breaking apart the family." Many children are shielded from the truth by a parent who stays silent in an attempt to "protect" them. Admitting that a parent is abusive toward the other parent can be an almost impossible truth to face. It's not your fault. Abuse is inexcusable.

Taking the Next Step

If you find yourself newly widowed, know that you are not alone. Grief is heavy, but growth and confidence are possible. *The Widow's Journal* by Carrie P. Freeman, PhD, can be a strong starting point to help you process loss and rebuild your footing.

If you are the primary provider in your household, do not carry the weight alone. Invite your spouse to participate in financial conversations and decisions. True provision is not just about leaving money behind; it is about leaving clarity, confidence, and peace of mind.

I challenge every couple to:

- Talk openly about your financial goals, even when perspectives differ.
- Share where important documents are kept and who the key advisors are.
- Involve both spouses not only in the numbers, but also in the vision for how your wealth will be used, protected, and passed on.

The *Key People and Documents Worksheet* is available online and provides a practical way to get started. Complete it together. Treat it as a guide so that no one you love is ever left saying, *"I don't even know where to begin."*

If you are an adult child or loved one, **stay attentive**. Be aware of the signs of financial, emotional, or physical abuse. Sometimes the people closest to us carry hidden burdens, and your awareness may be the first step toward safety and healing.

If you recognize yourself in these patterns, please know you are not alone. **Safe options do exist**. In some cases, even a temporary stay at a shelter can provide protection, clarity, and a first step toward freedom. You do not have to walk this path alone. Grief counselors, therapists, and professionals who specialize in family trauma can also provide support in ways that friends and family may not be able to. They create space for you to be heard, understood, and guided without judgment, and they can help you build a healthier path forward.

For confidential support, call the **National Domestic Violence Hotline at 1-800-799-7233** or text **"START" to 88788**. Trained advocates can connect you to resources, help you think through your options, and remind you that your safety and dignity matter.

Why Grief Feels Like Losing Part of Yourself

Grief is not just emotional; it's physical. Caregivers and spouses don't just give their time and energy; over months or years, their very bodies begin to adapt to the rhythms of the person they love. That's why, when death finally comes, it doesn't feel like losing someone else; it feels like losing a part of yourself.

Science helps explain why. Modern research shows that the bonds we form are more than sentimental; they are biological. Our brains, hormones, and even heartbeats sync with those closest to us. And when that synchrony is suddenly broken, the grief can be as much neurological as it is emotional.

What Happens at Death: The Caregiver's Body and Brain

When someone dies, it isn't only their body that changes. Those who were most deeply connected, especially caregivers and spouses, often undergo a physiological shift of their own.

Modern neuroscience shows that human beings don't just bond emotionally; we bond biologically. Over time, our nervous systems begin to "sync up" with the people we are closest to.

- Mirror neurons: These specialized brain cells fire both when we act and when we observe another person acting. They are part of why we yawn when someone else yawns or feel anxious when a loved one is anxious. In caregiving, mirror neurons are constantly engaged, wiring the caregiver's brain to the rhythms of the one they serve.
- Hormonal bonding: Oxytocin (sometimes called the "bonding hormone") and cortisol (the stress hormone) rise and fall together between spouses, parents, and children, and even caregivers and patients. This creates a shared emotional and physiological baseline.
- Brainwave synchrony: Research on couples and close teams shows that their brainwaves, heart rates, and breathing patterns literally fall into rhythm. This is why longtime spouses sometimes "sense" what the other is thinking, or why a caregiver knows when to check on a patient before an alarm goes off.

So, when death comes, it is not just an emotional shock; it is a neurological rupture. The synchrony is suddenly broken.

That's why caregivers often report:

- Phantom experiences: waking at night to listen for breathing, reaching for medications that no longer need to be given.
- Physical collapse: weeks or months of exhaustion, illness, or stress disorders once the caregiving role ends.
- Identity disorientation: feeling like part of themselves has been lost, because in a biological sense, it has.

In grief counseling, this is sometimes described as "losing half of your nervous system." The routines, the rhythms, even the brain chemistry that had adapted to another person's needs are now unanchored. The caregiver is left to relearn how to live in their own body without that constant tether.

This is why a caregiver's grief is so unique. It is not just about mourning the person who is gone. It is about rewiring the body, the brain, and the heart after losing the synchrony of a relationship that had become almost physiological.

Recalibration After Loss: Best Practices for Self-Care

Understanding the science of synchrony helps explain why the loss feels so destabilizing. But it also points us toward practices that can help the body and brain recalibrate after the bond is broken.

1. Restore your rhythms
Research shows that regular exercise, consistent sleep patterns, and even paced breathing can help reset the nervous system. Rhythmic activities like walking, swimming, or yoga are potent because they mimic the synchrony your body has lost while anchoring it in your own rhythm.

2. Reconnect socially
Loneliness amplifies grief. Studies of bereaved spouses and caregivers show that isolation increases the risk of depression, while regular social contact helps rebuild oxytocin pathways and stabilize mood. Even small steps, such as having a coffee with a friend, attending a

support group, or participating in worship or community events, can create new bonds that help rewire the nervous system.

3. Engage the brain
Caregiving often narrows life to routines of survival. After a loss, the brain requires novelty to regenerate and grow again. Learning a new skill, such as reading, playing a musical instrument, or volunteering, stimulates neuroplasticity: the brain's ability to form new connections and patterns of meaning.

4. Allow the full spectrum of emotion
Grief isn't only about sadness. Many caregivers feel relief, joy, or even freedom once their loved one has passed, and that is normal. It doesn't mean they loved less. It means they carried a heavy burden, did their best, and now their body and spirit are exhaling. Research on caregiver bereavement confirms that mixed emotions are healthy and often signal resilience.

5. Seek professional support
Therapists, grief counselors, clergy, or caregiver support groups can offer both validation and tools for healing. In some cases, professional care is not optional, especially if physical symptoms of grief (like insomnia, panic, or depression) interfere with daily life.

You gave your best. You honored your loved one in ways many will never see. Now the work is about honoring yourself by giving your body and brain the space, compassion, and time they need to heal.

Clarity Affirmations

- Now I know grief has many faces, and that's okay.
- I can give myself time and permission to feel what I feel.
- I can ask for help and let others carry some of the weight.
- I will delay big financial decisions until I have support and clarity.

- I will honor my loved one in ways that fit our values and resources.
- I will carry hope, even amid grief.

Action Steps (Grief First, Logistics Later)

1. **Tell** one trusted person, "You're my point of contact," and let them coordinate calls/meals/updates.
2. **Choose** a simple plan for the service or memorial that fits your faith, culture, and budget.
3. **Secure** immediate needs: dependents, pets, home, medications, and important mail.
4. **Create** a "holding place" (folder or box) for documents and bills; do not sort deeply yet.
5. **Keep** a small notebook (or phone note) of who called, what was promised, and what's pending.
6. **Set** a "no major money moves" window (e.g., 60–90 days) unless a professional advises otherwise.
7. **Book** support: clergy/therapist/grief group; schedule two short check-ins with close family.
8. **Protect** your body: sleep, water, a daily walk, simple meals. Grief is physical.
9. **Schedule** brief orientation calls with your attorney/financial advisor seeking information only, no decisions.
10. **Choose** one small daily ritual to remember your loved one (prayer, journal, photo, song).

Final Thoughts

Grief doesn't follow rules. It comes in waves of love, anger, relief, and regret, sometimes in the same afternoon. Let it. You don't have to "perform" strength or move on by a deadline. Say the names. Tell the stories. Accept help. Small, ordinary acts: sleep, food, a short walk, a friend's company are not detours; they're part of healing.

Clarity won't erase sorrow, but it can make room for it. When roles are clear and decisions are made at a pace that allows families to remember, families have the space to remember well. Permit yourself to go slowly, to feel what you feel, and to carry hope alongside the hurt.

CHAPTER FIFTEEN
After Death Part II: Logistics and Inheritance

"What you leave behind is not what is engraved in stone monuments, but what is woven into the lives of others."

Pericles

When a heart stops, two tracks begin: people and paperwork. The feelings won't wait, and neither will the forms. This chapter is about order: who to call, what to gather, what to do now, and what can wait.

We'll walk through the first days step by step and what to prioritize. We'll explain the difference between probate, trusts, and beneficiary designations, and outline how to handle accounts, property, taxes, and scams. You'll see how to keep the family informed, avoid rushed decisions, and prevent costly mistakes.

This isn't legal advice; it's a clear map to help you work with your attorney, CPA, and advisor without getting overwhelmed.

In this chapter, you'll learn:

- The first calls to make and documents to collect
- How probate and trust administration unfold
- How to retitle assets and handle retirement accounts
- A practical timeline for bills, taxes, and distributions
- Communication tips to reduce conflict and keep momentum

The Shift in Responsibility

It's important to understand that a **Power of Attorney ends at death**. Once a doctor declares the time of death, legal authority transitions to the **executor named in the Will** or the **trustee of the Trust**.

If those roles haven't been clearly established, the process can quickly become more complicated and stressful.

If you feel like everything is falling on you at once, remember: you don't have to keep it all in your head. At the back of this book, you'll find a **"What to Do After Death" worksheet**, a simple checklist you can follow, step by step, or hand to someone you trust.

It's there so you don't have to wonder, *"What comes next?"* in the middle of your grief.

A Note for the Caregiver

If you were the caregiver, the work doesn't stop when the heartbeat does. In some ways, it intensifies. People will expect you to:

- Make phone calls and notify relatives.
- Post updates or announcements on social media.
- Open your home to travelers arriving for the funeral.
- Cook meals or coordinate hospitality.
- Help plan the funeral or memorial.
- Answer questions you may not be ready for: *"How did they die?"*

People who weren't involved during the long months or years of caregiving may suddenly step forward with opinions about funeral details, estate matters, or "how things should be done." This can be overwhelming, even frustrating, when you are the one who carried the real weight in the final chapter of your loved one's life.

And sometimes, the burden falls on you not because you raised your hand, but because **no one else would.** Maybe your loved one refused to make decisions, clung to control, or resisted letting go. Maybe siblings stayed on the sidelines. By default, the role became yours.

If that's you, hear this: **you don't have to carry it all perfectly.** You don't need to do everything yourself. Delegate what you can: let others cook, write, or host. Lean on professionals for the technical details. Grief is not the time to prove strength; it's the time to allow help.

The Role of the Executor or Trustee

The executor (named in a Will) or trustee (named in a Trust) becomes the steward of what you've left behind. Their responsibilities include:

- Paying final expenses
- Filing a final tax return
- Distributing assets
- Closing accounts and notifying institutions
- Mediating between family members

This role can be an act of clarity or an invitation to crisis, depending on how well you've prepared.

When You Are Both Caregiver and Executor

Sometimes the same person is asked to do both: care for the one who is dying and then steward the estate once they are gone. It is a heavy double burden.

If that is your role, you may feel depleted, conflicted, or even resentful. You're grieving, but you're also being asked to manage forms, deadlines, and family expectations. You're expected to be both the heart and the head of the family.

If no one else stepped up before, they may step in now, but with opinions, not with help. That dynamic is real, and it's hard.

The best gift you can give yourself in this season is permission to share the load. Ask others to take one piece, however small. Let the attorney, the CPA, and the advisor carry the technical details. Let a friend handle phone calls or errands. You are not failing by asking for help; you are making space to breathe.

What Happens First

What the Law Requires After Death

While grief is ever-present, there are still legal steps to take:

- **Obtain the death certificate** (you'll need several copies)
- **Contact the funeral home** or cremation provider
- **Notify Social Security** and stop benefits
- **Begin estate administration** with the executor or trustee
- **Settle outstanding debts and final expenses**

The first few days after death are some of the most overwhelming in a family's life. Here is what usually happens:

Immediate Steps

1. Obtain the death certificate from the hospital or funeral home (order multiple copies for banks, insurance, Social Security, and other institutions).
2. Notify family and close friends.

3. Contact the funeral home or cremation provider.
4. Publish an obituary, if desired.

Notifications and Claims

5. Notify financial professionals (advisor, accountant, attorney).
6. Contact pension or annuity providers.
7. File life insurance claims.
8. Notify Social Security to stop or change benefits.

Estate and Final Affairs

9. Locate the estate plan (Will, Trust, Powers of Attorney).
10. Begin estate administration with the executor or trustee.
11. Settle outstanding debts and final expenses.

Financial Realities

Even after someone passes, the **estate's financial obligations continue**. These may include:

- Funeral costs (unless prepaid)
- Final medical bills
- Mortgage or rent
- Credit card balances and utilities
- Car payments
- Legal and probate fees

These must be paid by the estate before **any assets can be distributed** to heirs. Creditors get priority. If Medicaid was used for long-term care, a **Medicaid recovery review** may be initiated to recoup funds.

Probate and Legal Filings

As we saw earlier, probate is the court-supervised process of validating a Will and settling an estate. Some assets flow directly to beneficiaries; others must pass through probate.

Avoiding probate means fewer delays, lower costs, and more privacy. But if your plan is unclear, a crisis may unfold in public.

Probate vs. Non-Probate Transfers

Some assets pass **automatically** to beneficiaries. Others must go through probate, a court-supervised process that validates a Will and settles an estate.

Avoiding probate often means less delay, lower costs, and more privacy.

Assets That Typically Avoid Probate:

- IRAs, 401(k)s, and life insurance (with named beneficiaries)
- Jointly titled real estate (with rights of survivorship)
- Transfer-on-death (TOD) or payable-on-death (POD) accounts
- Assets held in a revocable or irrevocable trust

Assets That Typically Require Probate:

- Individually titled property without a beneficiary
- Bank accounts without TOD or POD
- Vehicles or personal items not held in trust
- Any asset without clear ownership transition

If you're not sure which of your assets fall into which category, review your titling, beneficiary forms, and estate documents now, before they're needed.

If you're the **trustee**, notify the estate attorney immediately to begin the process of asset distribution in accordance with the trust document.

Tax Considerations After Death

Death does not end taxes. It changes them.

- A **final income tax return (1040)** must be filed.
- An **estate income tax return (1041)** may be required.
- A **federal estate tax return (706)** is required for larger estates.
- Heirs may face **capital gains** or **income taxes** on inherited accounts.

If you've structured things well, much of this is simplified. If not, grief is compounded with tax surprises.

It's vital to choose someone trustworthy, organized, and capable of handling sensitive conversations.

The Final Tax Return (Form 706)

The executor is responsible for filing the deceased's **final federal estate tax return**. This includes:

- Assets transferred at death
- Any income earned during the final year
- Use of the **Deceased Spouse Unused Exemption (DSUE)**, which allows any unused estate tax exemption to be transferred to a surviving spouse

Work with a CPA or estate attorney to ensure everything is handled accurately.

Asset Valuation and the Alternate Valuation Date (AVD)

You'll need to assign a value to all assets in the estate, either:

- On the **date of death**, or
- Using the **Alternate Valuation Date**, which is six months later

Exceptions: Some assets (such as copyrights) must be valued as of the date of death. If an asset is sold before AVD, it's valued on the sale date. These decisions impact the **gross estate value** and taxes due.

Inheriting Assets: What You Need to Know

This is when I often meet caregivers, after the long journey of decline has ended, and now, they face the practical reality of what's left behind. Whether there's little or a lot, you need a plan.

Your two goals now should be:

1. Ensure you can live comfortably (retire, downsize, simplify)
2. Establish your own care and estate plan to prevent passing along similar burdens

Retirement Accounts

The rules for inherited retirement accounts depend on three main factors:

1) Whether or not you are the spouse, an **Eligible Designated Beneficiary, or an Ineligible Designated Beneficiary**

2) If the account is tax-deferred, such as a **Traditional IRA**, or if the account is a **Roth IRA**. It does not

matter whether it was an individual account or a workplace account (401(k), 403(b) 457(a), SEP or SIMPLE).

3) If the deceased had begun **Required Minimum Distributions**

Professional Note: The IRS rules for beneficiary IRAs can be complex through the IRS tax codes, so consult with a tax professional on your specific situation. The rules are too lengthy to summarize here sufficiently.

Pensions

Pensions are unique, specifically Defined Benefit pensions, because the transfer will depend on the structure of the pension plan rules and the options selected by the employee. The payout amount of the pension depends on which survivor option is selected. Options include:

- 100% life benefit (no benefit to survivors).
- 100% joint life benefit (for the employee and a spouse). The monthly payout is typically reduced significantly in this case.
- Partial joint benefit (50% to the surviving spouse). The payout is reduced, but less than with the 100% benefit.

If you have a workplace pension, it is very important to weigh your options. For other pensions, such as Cash Balance plans, the balance can be transferred to a beneficiary.

Transferring Investments

When investments are transferred to you, they may not align with your personal goals or risk tolerance. The deceased may have held:

- CDs, money market funds
- Concentrated stock positions (e.g., 100% Ford stock)

You're not required to keep these. However, many heirs struggle with the **"endowment effect,"** the emotional belief that selling a loved one's stock is like letting go of them. Be aware of this emotional pull, but evaluate the holdings rationally.

Life Insurance

Life insurance proceeds are **tax-free** and do **not need to be reported on your tax return**. This money can help with funeral expenses or provide peace of mind as you settle the estate.

Brokerage Accounts

For non-retirement brokerage accounts:

- **You receive a step-up in basis**: The cost basis is adjusted to the asset's value at the date of death (or AVD)
- Capital gains are only taxed on growth after death, not the entire appreciation

Example:
Dad bought Microsoft in 1980 at $4 per share.
At the time of death, it was worth $400/share.
Your new basis is $400/share, creating potentially significant tax savings when you sell.

Real Estate

Inherited homes and properties also receive a **step-up in basis**. For example:

- Your parents bought a house for $150,000
- At death, it's worth $600,000
- You inherit it at $600,000, and no capital gains are due on the appreciation up to that amount

Business Interests

If you inherit part or all of a business, it also receives a **step-up in basis**. The valuation used becomes your cost basis for future sale or transfer.

If you were a partner, your share continues. The deceased partner's interest passes to their heirs or, in the case of a buy-sell agreement, to the other party.

Trust Distributions

If you're a **beneficiary of a trust**, here's how taxes apply:

- Income distributions to you are **taxable at your personal income rate**
- Principal (or "corpus") distributions are **not taxable**

The trust should provide you with a **Schedule K-1** to include on your return.

What Else is Left?

When the paperwork is settled and the accounts are adjusted, what remains is bigger than numbers. It's the question of legacy. What will your loved ones carry forward: confusion or clarity, conflict, or peace?

That's why the work of preparing for what comes after has never been about documents alone. It's about what you leave *in* people, not just what you leave *to* them.

At this point, it's easy to feel buried in technical details: distributions, tax returns, and legal filings. Here's the truth: money is never just money. Every account, every distribution, every signature carries emotional weight. An inheritance can feel like provision, or it can feel like pressure. It can bring families together or drive them apart.

That's why we must step back from numbers and talk about what truly remains after death: **your legacy, and the relationships that carry it forward.**

Legacy Beyond Money

Legacy is not what is carved in stone, but what is written into the hearts of those you love.

- Letters.
- Videos.
- A blessing whispered in a child's ear.
- A family mission statement.
- A charitable act that outlives you.

Money sustains life. Legacy sustains meaning. Both matter.

These tools don't require vast wealth. They require intention.

If you want to be remembered for more than what you owned, take the time now to craft a message that will live on after you.

Avoiding Family Conflict

Even with a clear plan, emotions can run high after a death. That's why your documents and your communication matter so much.

Familiar sources of tension include:

- Perceived unfairness in distributions
- Disagreements about funeral arrangements
- Suspicion or blame directed at executors or caregivers
- Lack of communication during the process

You can't control every emotion, but you can reduce confusion and increase clarity. Strategies include:

- Holding a family meeting while alive
- Explaining decisions clearly and compassionately
- Using a third-party trustee or corporate fiduciary if needed
- Providing written guidance and context for heirs

Clarity Affirmations

- Now I know who does what: the executor, the trustee, and the advisors each have a role.
- I can follow a simple sequence instead of doing everything at once.
- I understand that careful records protect me and the estate.
- I will coordinate with an attorney and CPA before making irreversible moves.
- I will align new assets with a plan that fits my life, not my stress.
- I will update my own documents, so my family won't have to guess.

Action Steps (Essential Sequence)

1. **Notify core parties:** funeral home, immediate family, employer (if applicable), attorney, financial advisor, life insurer, and Social Security (the funeral home often reports to the Social Security Administration).
2. **Order death certificates:** 10–15 originals are common (banks/insurers often require them).
3. **Locate documents:** Will/Trust, POAs (now expired), deeds/titles, insurance, account statements, beneficiary forms, tax returns.

4. **Open the estate/Trust file:** meet the estate attorney to confirm probate vs. trust administration; set up an **estate or Trust bank account**, and keep receipts.

5. **Stabilize cash flow:** keep essential bills paid (utilities, mortgage, insurance) from the estate/Trust. Avoid using personal funds when possible.

6. **Insurance & benefits:** file life insurance claims; review employer benefits; stop automatic payments/benefits that must end.

7. **Accounts & titling:** retitle joint/TOD/beneficiary accounts; update deeds and vehicle titles per the Will/Trust.

8. **Inherited retirement accounts:** before moving anything, confirm your status (spouse vs. non-spouse) and the current IRS distribution rules (e.g., spousal rollover option; many non-spousal heirs face a 10-year window).

9. **Investments:** with your advisor, set a temporary low-risk posture if needed; avoid new, complex products while grieving.

10. **Taxes:** Coordinate with a CPA to file the final tax return; estate/Trust Form 1041 if required; discuss step-up in basis, Medicare IRMAA implications, and (if applicable) estate tax/DSUE.

11. **Real property & personal items:** follow the will/trust for distributions; document decisions to reduce disputes.

12. **Create (or refresh) your plan:** update your Will/Trust, POAs, beneficiaries, and a one-page estate map; set a reminder to review every 2–3 years or after significant life changes.

Short note for readers: Laws and timelines vary by state. These steps are educational; work with an estate attorney and CPA to tailor them to your situation.

Final Thoughts

After a death, paperwork and people intersect. Order is love in a practical form. Clear roles, clean records, and patient timelines turn potential conflict into cooperation. This is not a sprint. Make the next right decision, then the next, aligned with the documents, the law, and the values you share.

Fair doesn't always mean equal; transparency beats surprise. Work with your attorney, CPA, and advisor to avoid big, irreversible moves and keep communication open. Settle well, then use what you've learned to strengthen your own plan. The legacy you finish today becomes the calm your family stands on tomorrow.

Closing Remarks

"A good man leaveth an inheritance to his children's children."

Proverbs 13:22 (King James Version)

Throughout this book, we've explored the realities of aging, caregiving, and legacy. Together, we've walked through how to approach retirement with purpose, prepare for caregiving and extended care, minimize taxes, and preserve your legacy with clarity. Along the way, we've seen how finances, healthcare, and relationships are intricately intertwined, and how planning can help reduce confusion, conflict, and crisis.

Each chapter was designed not just to inform, but to encourage action. Planning doesn't erase pain or prevent every problem; it does bring direction. It transforms panic into a path, and it gives your family one less storm to weather.

It Was Never Just About the Money

That's the central truth of this book.

Money matters, but clarity matters more. Without it, even great wealth can leave a trail of crisis. With it, even modest means can create peace, direction, and blessing for generations.

True wealth goes far beyond net worth. It's found in your:

- Time
- Relationships
- Health
- Values

- Faith
- Character
- Impact

When you begin to view aging through this lens, your decisions change. You stop simply trying to avoid mistakes and start intentionally building something that will last.

That's the kind of wealth that endures.

What Comes Next

Here are five ways to take what you've learned and begin weaving clarity into your family's story, starting within the next 30 days:

1. **Schedule a family meeting**
   Use this book to spark meaningful conversations. Let your loved ones know what matters most to you.
2. **Meet with a licensed professional you can trust**
   Connect with a CFP®, estate attorney, or elder law expert who can help integrate your financial, legal, and healthcare goals.
3. **Write a legacy letter or family blessing**
   Pass on your values, lessons, and hopes, not just your assets.
4. **Review your key documents**
   Ensure your Will, Power of Attorney, beneficiary designations, and asset titles reflect your current wishes.
5. **Keep going**
   Planning isn't a one-time task; it's a lifestyle of stewardship and intentional living.

A Final Word

You don't need to have everything figured out. You just need to begin.

Every conversation, every update, every step forward is a gift to the people you love. It's a gift of direction. A gift of clarity. A gift of peace.

That is the power of preparation.
That is what it means to leave a legacy.
That is what it means to live with *Clarity Before Crisis.*

Benjamin Bolen, CFP®
Author, Planner, and Companion in the Journey of Aging

Glossary of Terms

Asset Protection

Strategies to protect wealth from taxes, creditors, or legal judgments.

Beneficiary

A person designated to receive assets or benefits from accounts, trusts, or insurance policies.

Caregiving

Providing physical, emotional, or logistical care to someone who is aging, disabled, or ill.

Charitable Giving

Donating money or assets to organizations or causes for philanthropic purposes.

DAF (Donor-Advised Fund)

A charitable giving account offering immediate tax benefits and flexibility in giving.

Drawdown Strategy

A plan for how to withdraw money from retirement accounts in a tax-efficient way.

Estate Planning

The process of arranging for the management and disposal of a person's estate during life and after death.

Executor

A person named in a Will to manage the estate and carry out the deceased's wishes.

Family Meeting

A gathering to discuss key issues such as caregiving, estate planning, or legacy wishes.

Fiduciary

A person or organization legally bound to act in another's best financial interest.

Financial Advisor

A professional who helps clients manage their finances and plan for the future.

Grief

Emotional suffering caused by loss, especially after the death of a loved one.

Hospice

Care focused on comfort for those near the end of life, rather than curing illness.

IRA (Individual Retirement Account)

A type of savings account with tax advantages for retirement.

Inheritance

Assets received from a deceased person.

Legacy

What you leave behind for others, including values, assets, and memories.

Long-Term Care

Services that support medical and personal needs for people with chronic illness or disability.

Medicaid

A joint federal and state program that helps with medical costs for people with limited income and resources.

Medicare

A federal health insurance program primarily for people aged 65 and older.

Medigap

Private insurance that covers gaps in Medicare, such as copayments and deductibles.

Nursing Home

A residential care setting that provides 24/7 support, supervision, and medical services for those who need help with daily living or ongoing health conditions. Designed to offer both comfort and clinical care, nursing homes support residents with a combination of skilled nursing, personal assistance, and a sense of community.

Power of Attorney

A legal document that gives someone authority to act on your behalf in financial or medical matters.

Probate

The legal process through which a deceased person's Will is validated and their estate is distributed.

QCD (Qualified Charitable Distribution)

A tax-free distribution from an IRA directly to a charity for those over age 70½.

RMD (Required Minimum Distribution)

The minimum amount you must withdraw from your retirement accounts each year, starting at age 73.

Retirement

The phase of life after one stops working full-time, typically relying on savings and benefits.

Roth IRA

A retirement account where contributions are taxed up front but withdrawals are tax-free.

Social Security

A federal program that provides retirement, disability, and survivor benefits.

Tax Planning

The analysis and arrangement of a person's financial situation to minimize tax liability.

Trust

A legal entity created to hold assets for the benefit of certain persons or entities.

Will

A legal document expressing a person's wishes about how their property is to be distributed after death.

Recommended Resource List

Websites:

- **AARP**: Resource library for retirees
- **SSA.gov**: The Social Security Website
- **Caring.com**: Senior living comparisons
- **Caregiving.com**
- **The Conversation Project**: End-of-life discussion guides

Books:

- *Being Mortal* by Atul Gawande
- *I Will Teach You to be Rich* by Ramit Sethi
- *Traction* by Gino Wickman
- *Start Thinking Rich* by Dr. Brad Klontz and Adrian Brambila
- *The 5 Types of Wealth* by Sahil Bloom
- *Mind Over Money Management* by Robyn Crane
- *The Psychology of Money* by Morgan Housel
- *Atomic Habits* by James Clear
- *The Next Conversation* by Jefferson Fisher
- *No Regrets* by Matthew Kelly
- *Eat, Drink, and Be Healthy* by Dr. Walter C. Willett, MD, PHD
- *Life on Purpose* by Victor J. Strecher

Additional Disclosures and Disclaimers

Financial Professional Disclosure:

Securities and advisory services are offered through LPL Financial (LPL), a registered investment advisor and broker-dealer (member FINRA/SIPC). Insurance products are offered through LPL or its licensed affiliates. University Bank and University Investment Services **are not** registered as a broker-dealer or investment advisor. Registered representatives of LPL offer products and services using University Investment Services, and may also be employees of University Bank. These products and services are being offered through LPL or its affiliates, which are separate entities from, and not affiliates of, University Bank or University Investment Services. Securities and insurance offered through LPL or its affiliates are:

Not Insured by FDIC or Any Other Government Agency	Not Bank Guaranteed	Not Bank Deposits or Obligations	May Lose Value

Privacy Disclosure:

To ensure the privacy of individuals, certain names have been changed. Additionally, some details have been embellished for narrative impact.

Advice Disclosure:

The information provided in this book is for informational purposes only and should not be considered professional advice. Readers should consult with an attorney, tax advisor, financial advisor, or insurance agent regarding their specific circumstances.

Consult a physician for specific medical advice.

This book draws from real-life experiences, qualified, professional sources, and current data from industry organizations, academic research, and government reports. While it is not an academic textbook, the information is based on the author's CFP® training and ongoing research across financial, healthcare, and legal disciplines.

About the Author

Benjamin Bolen, CFP®, is a financial planner with a mission rooted in personal experience. After losing his father to brain cancer at an early age, Benjamin began to understand the deep connection between legacy, loss, and the choices we make. His own legacy began with seven years of service in the U.S. Army, where he witnessed both the honor of duty and the heartbreak of veteran suicide.

Today, Benjamin brings that same sense of purpose to his work as a CERTIFIED FINANCIAL PLANNER™ in Ann Arbor, Michigan. Through his independent planning practice, he guides families through life's most meaningful transitions, retirement, caregiving, estate planning, and legacy decisions, helping them prepare not just financially, but emotionally and relationally.

He lives in the quiet countryside of Manchester, Michigan, with his wife and two children, where conversations about faith, family, and the future are just as meaningful as financial plans.

Clarity Before Crisis provides a comprehensive, human-centered roadmap for navigating aging, caregiving, and legacy planning. Unlike traditional financial guides that focus solely on investments and wealth, this book integrates emotional readiness, family dynamics, and personal values, helping readers prepare for the real-life challenges of aging and ensure their legacy reflects more than just money.

www.ingramcontent.com/pod-product-compliance
Lightning Source LLC
LaVergne TN
LVHW051050210926
848486LV00001B/62

* 9 7 9 8 2 9 5 5 3 3 7 4 7 *